playing

compass

Christian Explorations of Daily Living

David H. Jensen, Series Editor

Playing
James H. Evans Jr.

Shopping
Michelle A. Gonzalez

Forthcoming Volumes

Working
Darby Kathleen Ray

Eating and Drinking
Elizabeth Groppe

Parenting
David H. Jensen

playing

James H. Evans Jr.

Fortress Press
Minneapolis

BT709
.E93
2010
0496965899

PLAYING
Compass series
Christian Explorations of Daily Living

Cover design: Laurie Ingram
Book design: Christy J. P. Barker

Library of Congress Cataloging-in-Publication Data

Evans, James H., 1950-
  Playing / James H. Evans, Jr.
      p. cm. — (Christian explorations of daily living) (Compass series)
   Includes bibliographical references (p.   ).
   ISBN 978-0-8006-9726-6 (alk. paper)
  1. Play—Religious aspects—Christianity. 2. African Americans—Religion. I. Title.
   BT709.E93 2010
   233'.5--dc22

                          2010011885

The paper used in this publication meets the minimum requirements of American National Standard for Information Sciences—Permanence of Paper for Printed Library Materials, ANSI Z329.48-1984.

Manufactured in the U.S.A.
14 13 12 11 10 1 2 3 4 5 6 7 8 9 10

contents

foreword

Everyday practices matter for Christian faith. Our ordinary routines—eating, cooking, working, walking, shopping, playing, and parenting—are responses to the life God gives to the world. Christian faith claims that the ordinary materials and practices of human life are graced by God's presence. Basic foodstuffs become the body of Christ in a shared meal; water becomes the promise of new birth as ordinary people gather in Christ's name; and a transformed household becomes a metaphor for God's reign. Bodies, baths, meals, and households matter to Christian faith because God takes these everyday practices and materials as God's own—blessing, redeeming, and transforming them so that they more nearly reflect the hope and grace that come to us in the midst of the everyday.

Christian faith does not flee from the everyday but embeds itself in daily, ordinary routines. This book series considers everyday practices as sites for theological reflection. When we pay close attention to everyday practices, we can glimpse classical Christian themes—redemption, creation, and incarnation—in new light. This book series does not attempt to *apply* classical doctrines to particular practices but to offer narratives of ordinary routines, explore how immersion in them affects Christian life in a global world, and imagine how practice might re-form theology and theology re-form practice.

The series also explores the implications of globalization for daily practices and how these ordinary routines are implicated—for good and for ill—in the often bewildering effects of an increasingly interconnected world. Everyday practices, after all, are the places where the global becomes local. We encounter globalization not in abstract theory but in the routine affairs of shopping at the corner grocery for food grown on the other side of the globe, maintaining friendships with persons on other continents, and working at jobs where workplace decisions ripple outward to seemingly distant neighbors. Daily practices put a human face on the complex phenomenon of globalization and offer one place to begin theological reflection on this phenomenon. Paying close attention to these practices helps unveil the injustice as well as the hope of a global world. Since unreflective and consumptive forms of these daily practices often manifest themselves in American consumer society, this series also offers concrete suggestions for how daily practices might be reconfigured to more nearly reflect the hope and justice that are given to the world by God's grace. If daily practices implicate our complicity in global injustice, they might also be sites to imagine the world alternatively.

Though each book displays an organization uniquely its own, every title in the series offers three common themes: (1) The books offer thick descriptions of particular practices in North American society. What do parenting, cooking, and dressing look like in American communities in the twenty-first century? (2) The books survey varied Christian understandings of each practice, summoning theological resources for enhanced understanding and critique of typical forms of practice. What have Christians said about eating, dreaming, and traveling throughout their history, and how do their reflections matter today? (3) The books offer a constructive restatement of each practice and explore how ordinary practices might reshape or sharpen beliefs and themes of Christian faith. How does attention to practice affect the way we understand Christian theology, and how does attention to theology affect the way we understand everyday practice? Each book shares the conviction that Christian life is best encountered (and often best understood) in the midst of the ordinary.

The authors of these volumes are members of the Workgroup in Constructive Theology, an ecumenical group of teachers and scholars that writes and teaches theology in dialogue with contemporary critiques of Christian traditions. We are diverse in theological and denominational orientation yet share the recognition that Christian theology has often been employed for abusive ends. Theological traditions have silenced women, people of color, the poor, and GLBT persons. Our constructive restatements of Christian practice, therefore, do not simply restate classical Christian traditions but question them as we learn from them. We listen to the past while we also critique it, just as we hope that subsequent generations will also criticize and learn from us. Because so many voices have been silenced throughout the church's history, it is essential that Christian theologians attend to voices beyond the corridors of ecclesial and social power. Outside these corridors, after all, is where Christian faith takes root in ordinary life. Though each of us writes theology somewhat differently—some with explicit schools of theology in mind, such as liberationist or womanist theology—we all share the conviction that theology *matters*, not simply for reflective life but for the life of the world. Christian theology, at its best, is one expression of life's fullness and flourishing. Our words, in other words, ought to point to a more abundant life of grace in the face of the death-dealing forces at work on an economically stratified and ecologically threatened planet.

We have written each book with a minimum of technical jargon, intending them to be read in a wide variety of settings. The books may be used in seminary and undergraduate courses, including introductions to theology, ethics, and Christian spirituality. Clergy will also find them useful as they seek brief yet substantive books on Christian life that will inform their work of preaching, counseling, and teaching. We also imagine that each text could be used in churches for adult education classes. Many Christians seek guides for how faith is lived but are disenchanted with conservative approaches that shun dialogue with the wider culture of religious diversity. This series offers a progressive, culturally engaged approach to daily practices, globalization, and Christian theology. We think that the books are as important in the questions they ask as in the answers they attempt.

Playing often connotes frivolity. We play when we have sufficient time and leisure or when we're simply tired of hard work. In this understanding, play is far removed from the serious labors that make life possible and sustainable. James Evans in this delightful study offers another view: playing lies at the heart of Christian faith in the triune God. Through a close examination of African American literature and experience, and a reexamination of basic doctrinal affirmations, Evans recovers play as a subversive and even revolutionary activity, a practice of faith that gives life in the midst of structures and authorities that suffocate. In this study, Jesus is the political, cultural, and religious player who redeems by changing the game so that it no longer excludes but instead gives life. God creates us for freedom in a field of play. The Spirit summons us toward God's reign where the freedom of play never ends. Playing, in this view, is hardly frivolous but the pulse of life itself. Evans invites us to play as we live and work. Enjoy his words as you, too, might begin to play again.

David H. Jensen

preface

As I write this reflection I am surrounded by an unchar-acteristic clutter. In my dotage I have become quite par-ticular about picking things up, a habit my wife finds amusing and a little strange. On the floor of the small room that euphemistically serves as my study or den or exercise room . . . lie a plastic golf set, several trucks, books, and a host of assorted items all bearing the like-ness of the Sesame Street character Elmo.

I haven't picked up these things because as long as they are on the floor, the biweekly visit of our only grandchild has not truly concluded. He was born on my birthday—June 17—in 2007 (which was also Father's Day that year). I walked into the hospital room where his mother, her mother, and my youngest son along with other relatives simply gleamed. As I approached I leaned over and gave the young mother, Stephanie, a kiss, and oblivious even to my spouse by my side, I approached, the new love of my life. I took him into my arms, my heart overflowing with joy and peace, and I just looked at him. I asked my son, Jumaane, about his name. Christian James Evans. From that moment a bond was formed between us that only recently and predictably has been superseded by his affection for "Nana," my wife, Linda.

Having the opportunity to watch Christian at play, to see his intellect develop and the distinctive characteristics of his approach toward life take shape, reminds me of how important play is to every significant human achievement. Christian's insistence on using objects for purposes other than those for which they were designed reminds me of the play that is at the heart of what Thomas S. Kuhn called "paradigm shifts." New discoveries are impossible without play, and wonder is impossible apart from joy. Christian's father became a golf prodigy at a very young age, and I credit my gift of plastic golf clubs presented to him on his second birthday as the key to his talent. Christian has such a set, presented to him in the near certainty that he would inherit his father's ability. (This is a curious faith, given that my son's ability certainly did not come from me.) I have to smile as Christian grips the golf club not with his hands together, the way that came naturally to his father, but hands apart, like a hockey player. He places the plastic ball at his feet and hits screaming slap shots into the living room. The implements are of secondary importance. With golf clubs in his hands, Christian plays hockey. Play is not given to us. Play is what we have. Play is what we are.

One of Christian's favorite toys is a box with pop-up heads, and the objective is to pound the heads with a toy hammer. As he grips the hammer, I am reminded that for him the hammer, designed as an instrument of work, has become something else altogether. It is tempting to think of play as the opposite of work, but this is not necessarily the case. As I watch Christian wielding the hammer with near complete abandon, it occurs to me that play is not the opposite of work; play is work without anxiety.

Perhaps this is what Karl Marx struggled with in his analysis of alienated labor. When labor is considered valuable only to the degree that it is considered useful, a kind of anxiety ensues. Even Martin Luther, monk and revolutionary, struggled with the anxiety of work. His great breakthrough was a kind of liberation from the anxiety of works righteousness. His three "solas" were attempts to fend off the anxiety of work, although he never embraced play in its fullest sense. His "sola fide" pointed to the internal source of play; his "sola scriptura" pointed to the external source of play; and his "sola gratia" pointed to the eternal source of play. Faith gives us the confidence to play.

The experience embedded in the script of our lives gives us a place to play. It is grace as surplus, overflow, unlimited that allows us to play forever. Luther's "solas," unfortunately, were accompanied by a tendency— perhaps a result of the monastic life—to go it alone. It was John Calvin who provided a needed corrective to Luther's "solas." Calvin emphasized that the anxiety associated with work, even the work of salvation, could not be overcome in isolation from others. Calvin's Geneva, with its staunch social contracts and collective obligations, addressed the alienation of individual pursuit of salvation but could not embrace play and thus relieve the anxiety associated with such efforts.

Christian has playmates, and I am acquainted with two of them. I am the primary real playmate. I am the one who must watch him with an affirming glance as he empties his toy box on the floor. I must hide any displeasure associated with the fact that I will have to pick up everything later. But Christian has another playmate. This playmate is not quite real but not quite imaginary either. This playmate is Elmo, of Sesame Street fame. I think that, because Elmo does not look like anything or anybody, the mind of the child can enter into an unmediated relationship. While Elmo does not look like anything or anybody, Elmo feels like a playmate. Elmo is engaging, always interested in whoever is present at the moment. Elmo is patient, always willing to stick with a task until satisfied. Elmo is red, a color that distinguishes but does not differentiate Elmo from others.

It is never long before Christian takes me by the hand toward my reclining chair, points to my notebook computer, insists that I sit down with him and computer in my lap, and says, "Elmo!" I find a video and place the headphones on him and he is quiet. Although he is quiet and still while Elmo does his thing, play is happening. The images and ideas and words on the screen scramble to find their place in the order of things. Surely there is something special about a red puppet that creates a safe and pure relationship with a toddler. I know that Christian's future playmates will be diverse. Some will turn out to be mean and others mannered. Some will be patient and others persistent. Bright red Elmo will give way to the realities of race, class, and gender. Christian's mother's family is Caucasian and his father's family is African American, so perhaps, in our time, the racial reality for him will be different from that which I experience. In spite of the disappointments that likely will come his way, I am hoping that something the elders used to say when infants smiled is true: "They are playing with angels."

I was on my way to see a friend and fellow church member about something totally unrelated to this reflection when I had one of those providential moments. I had on my mind the monograph that I had agreed to author in our series Christian reflection on everyday practices. I had either been assigned to or volunteered for, without thorough consideration, the topic of *play*. I was searching the data banks of my memory for a hook or a handle by which I could hoist myself up and pull myself into the subject matter. I remembered reading something about a theology of play while in graduate school and made a mental note to research that. At that moment I pulled into the parking lot and stared as if for the first time at the sign identifying the place where my friend worked. There it was: "The Strong Museum of Play."

This museum began as a world-famous collection of dolls. The benefactor, Margaret Woodbury Strong, was a wealthy but eccentric woman. (It has been my observation that when one is wealthy, the kinder and gentler appellation of eccentric is used. When one is not wealthy or well known, one is just plain old strange.) She collected dolls of every type and class. They ranged from the daintiest porcelain dolls to the Raggedy Ann and Andy types. They came from every country and culture imaginable. There were literally thousands of them. They had been encased in glass, and visitors were allowed to look at but not touch them. Ms. Strong left a sizable sum to support and advance this museum. Over the years the administration of the museum recognized that these dolls were meant to be played with. While it was impractical to allow people, especially children, to play with the dolls, everything else in the museum was restructured and reconceptualized to promote play among children. Children came and continue to come by the thousands for the hands-on experience of being able to touch and play with anything in the museum, with the exception of the doll collection. The doll collection was moved to an upper floor where they are preserved but rarely seen. To her credit, Ms. Strong's primary concern was not with the dolls but for the children. That is why the museum was initially known as the Strong Children's Museum.

Within the last three years, the leadership of the museum officially changed the name to the Strong Museum of Play. Its resident Ph.D.s have conducted research on the significance of play in our culture. As you enter the museum today, you are met with pithy quotations such as "Play is the highest form of research" (Albert Einstein) or "Life must be lived as play" (Plato). The providence deepens. As I met with my friend, who is a vice president for the museum, I informed him that I was going to be engaged in some research on this very topic. He excitedly turned to his file cabinet and produced a research paper, written by the academic staff on the philosophy of play, that undergirded the expansion of the vision of the museum. He also informed me that in late April of 2007 an international team of scholars, all working in the area of play, would be convening at the museum, and I was invited to attend.

As I left the museum, I knew I would be spending fruitful hours in this place trying to understand the theological significance of play by watching these children do what comes naturally for them. To my mind sprang the words of Jesus, "Unless you become like little children, you shall not see the kingdom of God." My mind began to fill from the bottom up with questions about the meaning of play in our everyday lives and how play helps us to *apprehend*, *embody*, and *express* God. The terms are intentional in the sense that they reflect the Trinitarian perspective on play in this book. God is the reality that is only encountered in the knowing—that is, the apprehension of God. Transcendence notwithstanding, God is not an object to be grasped but a subject to be known. This God is also embodied, although not as an idol or anything else of human manufacture. As our bodies are not made by us but given to us, so in Jesus the incarnate one, God is given to use and not made by us. This God who is known by us, and given to us, is also expressed through us. God as Spirit is ushered into us, and resides in us, and also proceeds from us. In this procession God is expressed into the world.

As I begin this project, some preliminary and inchoate questions emerge regarding the relationship between the practice of play and Christology. First, I wonder whether we have been taught from an early age not to play with Jesus. In the community in which I was raised, one did not approach anything religious, especially if you were a child, without the requisite reverence. Playing church, while sometimes tolerated, was most often frowned upon. However, in a kind of native trinitarian warning, we were told, "Your arms are too short to box with God," "Don't play with Jesus," and "Don't tempt or test the Holy Spirit." One readily notices how these admonitions all refer to aspects of play: competition, frivolity, and experimentation. While it certainly can be understood how these admonitions were warranted, given the tendency by persons outside of our community to take our religious practices and devotion lightly, I have a hunch that it was precisely the ability to play with Jesus that allowed our faith to grow and adapt to the ever-changing challenges of living in a hostile culture.

Play involves a wide range of activities and perspectives, from the random testing associated with arranging and rearranging building blocks to the determined attempt to master chess or golf. What is joyfully embraced as play in one context may be rejected as disrespectful in another. Is there something inherently theological about play? Is there such a thing as Christian play? Under what circumstances does play become revelatory? I must admit that these and a myriad of other questions dance across my mind at the oddest moments. As they chase one another, making contact in a game of conceptual tag, concealing and revealing themselves in an ideological game of hide-and-seek, I am comforted with the realization that they are just playing. But is Jesus playing too?

The work that follows is the result of an assignment undertaken as part of the effort of the Workgroup in Constructive Theology, a collection of scholars who are an extremely gifted and generative community. The assignment was to relate an everyday common practice to theological reflection. Play is such a practice. It has given me the opportunity to ponder something that we often take for granted and to ask what for me is the most important question: "What is the theological meaning of this practice?" Since for me theology is connected with life, the broader cultural and social dimensions of this practice also come into focus. I want to thank my colleagues in the workgroup for their encouragement. I also want to thank my colleagues at the Strong Museum of Play in Rochester, New York, for their hospitality and inclusion in their discussions of the meaning of play in our time. I especially want to acknowledge their provision of the thoughts on play presented in the quotations throughout the book. Special gratitude goes to Mr. Rollie Adams, president and CEO of the museum; my good friend, vice president of the museum, and member of the Saint Luke Tabernacle Community Church where I serve as senior pastor, Mr. Richard Battle; and the entire research and guest services staff for their support. Finally, I want to thank my wife, Linda, for her steadfast love. But best of all, this book is dedicated to my grandson, Christian James. May his childhood days be filled with pleasure and play.

the play's the thing

I'll have grounds
More relative than this—the play's the thing
Wherein I'll catch the conscience of the King.

Hamlet, act 2

The aim of this book is modest, and its structure is similarly simple. The student of theology will recognize its trinitarian framework. It is comprised of three extended chapters. The next chapter, "Playing in the Dark: God and the Field of Play," examines the notion of play as a basis for a Christian understanding of God. The third chapter, "Don't Hate the Player, Hate the Game: Jesus as a Player," explores what it means to say that "Jesus plays the field," based on the preliminary conclusions reached in chapter 2. The fourth chapter, "The Holy Spirit at Play: Humanity, Church, and the Cosmos," looks at the spontaneity traditionally thought to be at the heart of Christian pneumatology and the church in light of the notion of play. The postlude, "Playing around the World," treats in an admittedly cursory manner the notion of play as a global practice. What does the notion of play say about contemporary existence in a world where time and space are no longer insurmountable obstacles to community?

Before moving on to a fuller explication of these issues and questions in the chapters that follow, a conceptual overview of the idea of play as it relates to this project is in order.[1] The epigraph that begins this chapter is uttered by the protagonist in William Shakespeare's *Hamlet*. Hamlet, having been visited by a ghostly figure and told that his uncle, King Claudius, murdered his father, writes and presents a play. The purpose of this play is more than entertainment; it is an attempt to elicit the truth about the murder. It is in this context that Hamlet declares, "The play's the thing." While play, in this sense, refers to a dramatic literary work, play in the broader sense is connected to the desire to approach and appropriate reality in a distinctive way.

> Life must be lived as play.
>
> *Plato*
> *Greek philosopher*
> *427–347 BCE*

The idea of play is one that has been explored in a wide variety of disciplinary and historical contexts. From philosophy to psychology to sociology to literary theory to cultural studies and beyond, the idea of play has functioned as a central motif or theme. The near universality of play as a human practice makes a simple and definitive summary difficult if not impossible. Therefore, what is presented below is a limited but necessary attempt to provide a basis for conversation about play. Some of the major and exemplary thinkers and ideas related to play are presented as illustrations of a fundamental insight into the nature of play; that is, that play is an avenue to truth. The ideas explored here are presented along two axes; chronological order and thematic continuity. The assumption here is that play is best understood when its synchronic and diachronic dimensions are taken into account.

The Play of Man

At the beginning of the twentieth century, scientific interest in biology, zoology, and the emerging fields of psychology and sociology nudged the concept of play to the forefront of academic inquiry. Karl Goos, an early and influential scholar in the field, initially focused on the play of animals. However, it was when he turned his attention to the notion of play in humans that the full significance of the concept came into view. In his landmark work, *The Play of Man*, he examines this concept as foundational to two main human impulses.

The first is the impulse to experimentation, and the second is the impulse to imitation. In the transition from the study of animal behavior to the study of human behavior, Groos wrestles with the distinction between "instinct" and "impulse." Groos notes that when considering human play, "the word *instinct*, while generally applicable, is not universally so—a difficulty which is much more conspicuous here than in the classification of animal play. . . . The word *instinct* does not cover the

> It is a happy talent to know how to play.
> *Ralph Waldo Emerson*
> *American writer*
> *1803–1882*

ground with its commonly accepted definition as inherited association between stimuli and particular bodily reactions. . . . It is safer, therefore, to speak of such play as the product of 'natural or hereditary impulse.'"[2] These natural or hereditary impulses support the human need to experiment and to imitate. In experimentation human beings test their physical surroundings, perceptions, and conceptual assumptions. In imitation human beings seek to influence reality as we know it by replaying or re-creating the dramas of survival, courtship, and love. Groos concludes that play is at the heart of the physiological, bio-logical, psychological, aesthetic, sociological, and peda-gogical dimensions of human existence.

Homo Ludens

Johan Huizinga's seminal and controversial work on play continues to serve as a touchstone in the field of play stud-ies. Huizinga was a Dutch historian who died in occupied Holland in 1945. He was born into a Mennonite family of doctors and other professionals. He, however, observed that he was descended from "Baptist preachers and pro-vincial farmers." In his major work, *Homo Ludens: A Study of the Play Element in Culture*, he argues that play is a fundamental feature of human identity and des-tiny. Previous thinkers had established the categories of *Homo sapiens* (man the knower) and *Homo faber* (man the maker). For Huizinga, the human being as cognitive agent was insufficient and the human being as worker was a distortion. He notes that "play only becomes pos-sible, thinkable, and understandable when an influx of *mind* breaks down the absolute determinism of the cos-mos."[3] For Huizinga play is "a special form of activity . . . a well defined quality of action which is different from ordinary life."[4]

Here as in almost all scholarly treatments of play, the concept defies exact definition. Instead, Huizinga must content himself with a partial list of the characteristics of play. Play is voluntary, not ordinary or real life; play is secluded or limited; play creates or is order; play tends to surround itself with secrecy. While acknowledging that play has certain psychological and physiological dimensions, Huizinga focuses on the sociological and cultural functions of play. Sociologically speaking, play establishes and legitimates social order. It regulates the relations between social groups and classes and it allows individuals to negotiate the sociological playing field to their advantage. Culturally, play creates and transforms cultural ideas and artifacts. Through play the collective memory of the group is preserved and transmitted. Play permits the inherent conflicts within the group to be conducted and resolved without destroying the social fabric. Play also keeps the aims and goals of the group in view. Play reveals what is important to any given society. Huizinga observes:

> In our play we reveal what kind of people we are.
>
> *Ovid*
> *Roman poet*
> *43 BCE–17 CE*

It has not been difficult to show that a certain play-factor was extremely active all through the cultural process and that it produces many of the fundamental forms of social life. The spirit of playful competition is, as a social impulse, older than culture itself and pervades all cultural life like a veritable ferment. Ritual grew up in sacred play; poetry was born in play and nourished on play; music and dancing were pure play. Wisdom and philosophy found expression in words and forms derived from religious contests.

The rules of warfare, the conventions of noble living were built up on play-patterns. We have to conclude, therefore, that civilization is, in its earliest stages, played. It does not come *from play* like a babe detaching itself from the womb; it arises *in* and *as* play, and never leaves it.[5]

Huizinga, then, argues that play is more than what we occasionally do. It is essentially who we are.

Humans, Play, and Games

Roger Callois was at once an admirer and a critic of Huizinga's notion of play. Callois, a French sociologist, affirmed Huizinga's basic understanding of play as a free activity. However, his critique of Huizinga's understanding of play is that it is idealistic. That is, it deemphasized the political context of play. Contributing to this critique was an underlying suspicion that Huizinga did not examine the revolutionary potential of play while living under Nazi occupation. Callois argues that all play occurs in specific spatial and temporal contexts in which that freedom is exercised. Thus, Callois offers the following definition of play:

> *Free*: in which playing is not obligatory; if it were, it would at once lose its attractive and joyous quality as diversion; *Separate*: circumscribed within limits of space and time, defined and fixed in advance; *Uncertain*: the course of which cannot be determined, nor the result attained beforehand; and some latitude for innovations being left to the player's initiative; *Unproductive*: creating neither goods, nor wealth,

nor new elements of any kind; and, except for the exchange of property among the players, ending in a situation identical to that prevailing at the beginning of the game; *Governed by rules*: under conventions that suspend ordinary laws, and for the moment establish new legislation, which alone counts; *Make-believe*: accompanied by a special awareness of a second reality or of a free unreality, as against real life.[6]

In essence, Callois argues that one can understand play only within the context of a game. The game provides the formal necessities for play to occur. Games provide rules, time, and space for play.

Callois divides play into four distinct categories; agon (competition), alea (chance), mimicry (simulation), and ilinx (vertigo). Put another way, there are competitive games (most sports), games of chance (most forms of gambling), games of simulation (most video or virtual reality games), and cultural games in which either one's identity is masked or one's perception of reality is altered temporarily (make-believe and spinning until dizzy). These types of games proceed along an axis between *paideia*, the active, exuberant, and spontaneous play of children, to *ludus*, the calculated, contrived, and rule-bound play of adults. Callois moves on from the consideration of play in and of itself to play in the contexts of games. However, his

> Man is most nearly himself when he achieves the seriousness of a child at play.
>
> *Heraclitus*
> *Greek philosopher*
> *535–475 BCE*

> Almost all creativity involves purposeful play.
> *Abraham Maslow*
> *American psychologist*
> *1908–1970*

major contribution to play studies is his insistence on responding to the assertion that "play is a free activity" with the question, "Within what limits?"

Play as Rhetoric, Recapitulation, and Performance

Perhaps the most influential contemporary scholar in the field of play studies is Brian Sutton-Smith. Even after a long and brilliant career, Sutton-Smith still pursues the ever-elusive understanding of play:

> In forty years of pursuing the meaning of play, it has become apparent to me than an understanding of play's ambiguity requires the help of multiple disciplines. But it has also become apparent that it is difficult to approach the subject matter of play directly when there is so much implicit ideological rhetoric that comes with these disciplines. The procedure to be adopted, therefore, is like that of Umberto Eco in his novel, *The Name of the Rose* (1983), in which he describes the activity of a group of medieval monks who, having realized that it is impossible to say what God is, have devoted themselves to revealing what God is *not*. And so the margins of their hand-printed Bibles are replete with artistic playfulness exhibiting nonsensical creatures that could not have existed and actions that are impossible. . . . I attempt to arrive at the meaning of play in a sometimes similarly indirect and nonsensical fashion.[7]

Sutton-Smith observes that the sometimes bewildering assortment of perspectives on play is due to its inherent ambiguity. Most people know what play is when they encounter it, but describing it in a concise way is another matter altogether. It is this very ambiguity in the idea of play that resists theoretical precision. Instead, Sutton-Smith suggests a rhetorical approach. That is, the various dimensions of play demand or require a particular way of talking about them. Drawing on the work of Kenneth Burke, Ludwig Wittgenstein, and T. S. Kuhn, Sutton-Smith concludes that the rhetoric of play must be attributed to the character of play itself.

Subsequent to his work on play, ambiguity, and rhetoric, Sutton-Smith revisits the theory that play is a type of reenactment of some basic social or evolutionary drama. He observes that "the classic recapitulation theories foster the view that individuals in their development (ontogeny) go through stages similar to those gone through biologically by earlier species (phylogeny)."[8] In contrast to those understandings of play that emphasize its character as a radically free activity conducted in the rarified air of novelty, play as recapitulation emphasizes play as a re-creation, rehearsal, or reenactment in which emotional balance is restored as conflicting emotions are allowed to play themselves out within the safe space of the imagination. Sutton-Smith concludes, "What this recapitulatory theory does for us, if valid, is to indicate that despite all our civilized progress, our play forms are still fundamentally what

> To the art of working well a civilized race would add the art of playing well.
>
> *George Santayana*
> *American philosopher*
> *1863–1952*

they have always been for mammals: contests (rivalry), celebrations (belonging), explorations (novelty), performances (display), and, for humans, playfulness (humor) and imaginings (mind play). They all continue, whether the old or the new forms, to recapitulate the novel balance between the primary and secondary emotions, which were a part of the mammal evolutionary passage."[9]

Beyond rhetoric and recapitulation, Sutton-Smith has also explored the notion of play as performance. In this sense, play—for example, between a mother and child, or two playmates, or even actors in a theatrical production for that matter—is a type of performance.[10] In all of these instances, the participants are permitted to be someone else. In certain social and political contexts, this type of play breaks normal social conventions. It permits the lower classes to play the part of social elites and creates space for social elites to be viewed as comic or farcical figures. Put another way, play is the context in which the first becomes last and the last becomes first.

From the latter part of the twentieth century on, scholars have developed and expanded the idea of play. Their basic premise is that the power of play is a constitutive and pervasive feature of human existence. Several writers have attempted to show how the idea of play is related to intellectual endeavors in a variety of fields.[11] While this brief overview of the concept of play has not been exhaustive but only suggestive, some of the central ideas and trajectories therein carry over into the body of this work.

The Structure of Play

Play is something we do every day. It is an everyday practice. As with most everyday practices, its deeper significance, the interstices of its relationship to other aspects of human existence, and its contextual character are often overlooked. Put another way, play has a theological character.

While the literature on the meaning of play is voluminous and we have merely sampled some of it here, it is important at this point to posit a working definition of play for the purposes of this study. *Play is a set of activities or practices that occurs in the interstices between freedom and structure, between the subject(ive) and object(ive), between creation and imitation.* First, one of the central features of play is freedom. To play means to engage in activities and practices in which boundaries are crossed and new space is discovered. However, one of the features that makes play pleasurable is the act of playing against something or someone. This is why most play takes place in the context of a game. That game is sometimes a given and sometimes it is constructed for the purposes at hand. But the freedom that gives play its dynamic is balanced by the structure that gives play its form. In its purest manifestation, play is both freedom and structure without distinction.

Second, play has both a subjective and an objective dimension. Play denotes a player, a subject, and something that is the object of play. This is why play often involves toys or instruments. Toys or instruments are not always

> Just play. Have fun. Enjoy the game.
>
> *Michael Jordan*
> *American basketball player*

designed to be such. The subject can convert anything (a cardboard box, the television remote control, a pot, or a tin can) into a toy or instrument.

Third, play has a creative and an imitative dimension. Play is an activity in which creativity is unleashed. New ways are made and new worlds are fashioned. Play frees us from the restrictions of the world in which we live. This is why play requires imagination. Play is also, however, an activity that is an imitation of the world. Play has a mimetic function.[12] In this sense, play connects us to the actual world in which we live. This is why play requires discipline.

As noted above, this work is comprised of three main chapters reflecting an obvious trinitarian structure. Yet theological discourse is contextual. The relationship of God, Christ, and the Holy Spirit to the idea of play has been framed in particular cultural language. So this book attempts to address a central question: What is the meaning of the practice of play, especially as seen in an African American cultural and theological context?

2

playing in the dark:
god and the field of play

It is not enough to rail against the descending darkness of barbarity. . . . One can refuse to play the game. A holding action can be fought. Alternatives must be kept alive. While learning the slow art of revolutionary patience.

South African poet Breyten Breytenbach

Play and Liminality

The free, spontaneous, pre-rational, and fictive dimensions of literature have long been recognized. Indeed, literature as a product of the human imagination is the "wild child" of philosophy (the search for truth) and poetry (the search for beauty). We discussed above the observation that play can be thought of as the structure of reality (Heraclitus's principle that "the course of the world is a child at play, moving figures on a board"). A corollary of this principle is that play is an essential feature of both the production and the criticism of literature. That is, literature is a ludic product, and analysis of it is ludic criticism.

In his splendid book *The Wreath of Wild Olive: Play, Liminality, and the Study of Literature*, Mihai I. Spariosu examines the ludic character of modern Western/European literature drawing on Victor Turner's concept of liminality.[1] Turner borrowed the term *liminality* from Arnold van Gennep, who in his book *Rites of Passage* (1908), describes the three stages of such a rite. While Turner is best known for his explication of liminality in more well-known works, it is in a lesser-known work, *From Ritual to Theatre: The Human Seriousness of Play* (1982), that the ludic dimensions of the concept are brought into focus. The three stages of a rite of passage are separation, transition, and incorporation. Spariousu notes, "Of particular interest here is the second stage of a rite of passage, the transitional or liminal stage. During this stage, the initiands experience a blurring of all social distinctions or a 'leveling' process."[2]

An important aspect of this liminal experience is that one is not only in the midst of a transition from one state to another; one experiences a range of social and personal possibilities that are virtually unlimited. Social, economic, and political boundaries are obliterated and the various pieces of one's existence are available for playful rearrangement.

> Whoever wants to understand much must play much.
>
> *Gottfried Benn*
> *German physician*
> *1886–1956*

Turner's observations on liminality are drawn principally from premodern societies. An important question is whether this attractive notion of liminality is achievable in modern, industrialized communities. It is, perhaps, in response to this kind of query that Turner draws a helpful distinction between "liminal" phenomena and "liminoid" phenomena.[3] The liminal experience is characterized by seriousness, obligation, compulsion, and even dread. The liminal stage in premodern rites of passage is serious business, not because there is no freedom involved but because there is so much at stake. The liminal stage is preparation for the serious business of an adult responsible existence. Here one is free to participate in the construction of the best of all possible worlds. That is, play is preparation for a new reality. Turner contrasts this with the liminoid experience. This experience is made possible by the leisure available in modern societies. So the liminoid experience is characterized by spontaneity, joy, frivolity, mimicry, and so on. The liminoid experience grows out of and is a response to a highly mechanized, bureaucratic, hyper-rational understanding of reality. The liminoid experience is escape from the harsh realities of everyday existence. Here one is free from the world as given.

Turner's notions can shed some light on the central problematic of this chapter: What does it mean (especially for African Americans but also for other Americans) to play in the dark as a radical, revolutionary act of resistance and re-creation?

Toni Morrison's *Playing in the Dark*

A work that has been inexplicably overlooked by the field of ludic criticism is Toni Morrison's intriguing text *Playing in the Dark*. In this brief but powerful work, she undertakes the task of uncovering a neglected feature in literature, especially American literature. Her focus is not merely the conscious and explicit roles black people play in the creation of literary texts but something much deeper. Morrison observes that her interests lie in the curious literary construction of "America" and how the black presence has been ever present though rarely acknowledged. She is interested "in the way black people ignite critical moments of discovery or change or emphasis in literature not written by them."[4]

Morrison's reading of Western literature reveals that "Americanness" has only achieved definition over and against an "Africanist presence." The two realities are so intertwined that Morrison wonders "whether the major and championed characteristics of our national literature—individualism, masculinity, social engagement versus historical isolation; acute and ambiguous moral problematics; the thematics of innocence coupled with an obsession with figurations of death and hell—are not in fact responses to a dark, abiding, signing Africanist presence."[5]

This Africanist presence—African people are rarely recognized as such in this literature—functions as a trope and "little restraint has been attached to its uses."[6] Literary criticism, Morrison argues, has attempted in various ways to deny, negate, and obliterate the significance of this presence. Yet it is this very black presence that may hold the key to understanding the complex process of racial identity formation and its relation to the national consciousness.

It is important to see how inextricable Africanism is or ought to be from the deliberation of literary criticism and the wanton, elaborate strategies undertaken to erase its presence from view. What Africanism became for, and how it functioned in, the literary imagination is of paramount interest because it may be possible to discover, through a close look at literary "blackness," the nature—even the cause—of literary "whiteness." What is it *for*? What parts do the invention and development of whiteness play in the construction of what is loosely described as "American"?[7]

The remainder of Morrison's text is devoted to an examination of the effects of the black presence upon the white mind. She is interested, of course, in the ways in which enslaved Africans resisted this conceptual entombment, but she is more interested in the effects of this racial ideology on the minds, hearts, and imaginations of the slaveholding class. What white writers do either when they consciously engage or unconsciously ignore the Africanist presence reveals more about them than it does their subject matter. The way in which white writers construe, fabricate, or invent the Africanist personae is what Morrison calls "an extraordinary mediation on the self; a powerful exploration of the fears and desires that reside in the writerly conscious."[8] Morrison concludes her narrative with the observation that "these deliberations are not about a particular author's attitudes toward race. That is another matter. Studies in American Africanism, in my view, should be investigations of the ways in which a nonwhite, Africanist presence and personae have been constructed—invented—in the United States, and of the literary uses this fabricated presence has served. . . . My project is an effort to avert the critical gaze from the racial object to the racial subject; from the described and imagined to the describers and imaginers; from the serving to the served."[9]

What then does it mean for Morrison—and for the rest of us—to play in the dark? It means, among other things,

> Play fosters belonging and encourages cooperation.
>
> Stuart Brown, MD
> Contemporary American
> psychiatrist

to attempt to construct a livable world in which the realities of race and racism continue to hold sway. Writers play. They play with words, ideas, sounds, symbols, and signs. Yet this play is not carried out in the purified air of freedom and noncontingency that is often claimed. American writers—and anyone who is engaged in the search for beauty and truth—are casting their paints against a canvas already darkened with the blood, sweat, and tears of an unacknowledged African people. Perhaps this is the reason that most Americans—some African Americans included—are incapable of seeing the backdrop against which their striving for happiness is set. In our living and dying, in our getting and spending, in our coming in and going out, we are arranging the chess pieces of our lives against a field of darkness. We are, in essence, playing in the dark.

> People tend to forget that play is serious.
>
> *David Hockney*
> *Contemporary British painter*

But Morrison's text does not suggest that all attempts at meaning-making are futile. On the contrary, even in the writing of this little book, she is at play. Her inspiration for this book was related to the most sublime form of musical play, a Louis Armstrong jazz performance. She notes that her project "rises from delight, not disappointment . . . from the way writers transform aspects of their social grounding into aspects of language, and the way they tell other stories, fight secret wars, limn out all sorts of debates blanketed in their text."[10] Perhaps it is the best hope for those of us who live in this historical experiment called the United States to come to terms with the reality of playing in the dark, and in doing so we might someday see the light.

Joseph Conrad's *Heart of Darkness*

Darkness is a trope that points to the inevitable and inescapable backdrop of fecundity, fear, chaos, and crisis that has shaped not only black literary production in the West but black life itself. Perhaps the most controversial and revealing portrait of this phenomenon is Joseph Conrad's *Heart of Darkness*, published in 1902. Appearing at the beginning of the twentieth century and only four years prior to W. E. B. DuBois's *The Souls of Black Folk*, Conrad's novel weaves a tale of a quest for an ivory dealer, Mr. Kurtz, who dared to venture into the center of the African continent. Kurtz dies there because he encounters "the horror" found only in the heart of darkness. While much of the critical commentary on this novel focuses on a psychological trek into the European mind, for our purposes, this novel provides an insight into the function of darkness as a literary field of play. This darkness is associated with the bravado of usurpers—"they were men enough to face the darkness"[11]—but it is also associated with violence:

> It was just robbery with violence, aggravated murder on a great scale, and men going at it blind—as is very proper for those who tackle a darkness. The conquest of the earth, which mostly means taking it away from those who have a different complexion or slightly flatter noses than ourselves, is not a pretty thing when you look into it too much.[12]

> This darkness is not just a passive backdrop for conquest but exacts a price on the European interlopers. It changes them not on the outside but on the inside, and for those who survive they must be persons "with no entrails."[13]

Otherwise the darkness leads to a madness of the soul.[14]

Within this darkness as Conrad describes it, black people are not seen as human but "nothing earthly now—nothing but black shadows of disease and starvation."[15] As the central characters of the story approach the interior of the continent, the possibility of perceiving these black shadows as human advances and then recedes. "The earth seemed unearthly. We are accustomed to look upon the shackled form of a conquered monster, but there—there you could look at a thing monstrous and free. It was unearthly, and the men were—No, they were not inhuman."[16] However, following this tacit acknowledgment of the humanity of Africans, they are referred to later in the novel as "dark human shapes . . . flitting indistinctly against the gloomy border of the forest."[17]

It is the recognition of this "thing monstrous and free" that is the key to hidden possibilities suggested by, though not recognized by, the text. Within the dank, dangerous, fearful, and obscure realm of the darkness, the opportunity to play exists. This play takes place behind a veil of darkness (compare with DuBois) and is often indistinguishable by outsiders from ordinary work. The description of the African working the boiler on the steamship (reminiscent of Ralph Ellison's paint engineer in *Invisible Man*) also employs indigenous religious implements to manipulate his identity as a mere worker to become one who is a player, that

> Deep meaning lies often in childish play.
>
> Johann Friedrich von Schiller
> German poet
> 1759–1805

is, able to arrange and rearrange his work according to his own game plan.[18] Even in the midst of danger these shadowy shapes are capable of "running bent double, leaping, gliding, distinct, incomplete, evanescent."[19] Although obscured by the veil of racism, it may well have been this ability to play in the dark that enslaved Africans brought with them to the New World.

Play, Slavery, and Freedom

One of the most poignant and enduring characteristics of the experience of enslaved Africans in the New World was their ability to find, ferret out, and fix their gaze on freedom. Among the strategies employed by enslaved Africans to open new and fresh space within the confines of confinement was storytelling, specifically the Brer Rabbit tales. Though the telling of these stories was initially thought to be a harmless diversion, they actually functioned as part of a broader cultural effort to mitigate the destructive, inhumane, and immoral effects of chattel slavery. A particularly helpful treatment of this aspect of slave existence is rendered by Riggins R. Earl Jr. in his much-overlooked work *Dark Symbols, Obscure Signs*.[20]

Significant for our purposes is the section of his work where he examines the relation between work, play, and God in these stories as part of the effort to break the chains of a hypocritical slaveholding ethic. Earl argues that the telling of these stories relativized the backbreaking labor of slavery through a kind of play. Through becoming "a playful worker," the enslaved African "creates what might be characterized as the 'ethical gap,' created when the conventional boundary between right and wrong is intentionally confused or reversed by the oppressed."

While the intentional actions causing confusion look like moral chaos to the oppressor, the oppressed see it merely as being the creative inversion or reversal of oppressive ethical logic."[21] Through this reversal enslaved Africans created an "ethic of playful versatility." Earl argues that Brer Rabbit's creativity is a demonstration of this ethic of playful versatility. "Brer Rabbit's genius as a *playful worker* symbolized the distinction that slaves needed to make between the worker as functionary and the intrinsic value of the being of the worker. . . . In the act of juxtaposition slaves came to see that both work and play as creative projects are dialectical in nature. They saw that the *playful worker* and the *working player* were dialectical sides of the same coin."[22]

Brer Rabbit is able to play because he has the freedom to do so. He is able to laugh and to express a fundamental enjoyment of life in spite of being physically weaker than his traditional adversaries, Brer Wolf and Brer Bear. Brer Rabbit is able to play because he has the courage to do so in the face of overwhelming odds, making the point that freedom is not for cowards. Brer Rabbit is the symbolic representation of the enslaved African (note that these tales are adaptations of traditional African stories involving a hare as the central character) and expresses a creative claim to freedom and joy in the midst of nearly impossible circumstances. As Earl notes, Brer Rabbit helped slaves redefine work psychologically by playing the spirit of work itself against the oppressive work structures (time and space) of the plantation world. As the playful worker, Brer Rabbit became for slaves the personification of the spirit of work itself. He knew how, as a playful worker, to turn work into play and play into work."[23]

But the telling of stories was not the only way that enslaved Africans employed playful strategies. Dwight N. Hopkins, in his highly acclaimed work *Down, Up, and Over: Slave Religion and Black Theology*, observes that the existence of enslaved Africans was dualistically divided between the period of "sunup to sundown" and "sundown to sunup." During the former period, the existence of the enslaved African was entirely controlled by the interests, demands, and desires of the slaveholders. "In the time and space from sunup to sundown white Protestant slave owners took the initiative to fashion former Africans into physically enslaved, spiritually stunted, and culturally subordinated African Americans."[24]

During these daylight hours the lives of enslaved Africans were totally conscribed by the institution of slavery. The time—sunup to sundown—and the space—the plantation—were marked by nonredemptive labor, because the slaveholding class built their understanding of the world on the puritanical principle of work as the primary means for humans to create and then subdue their world.[25] However, as related to the subject of this chapter, our interests lie in the period from sundown to sunup. This is the period in which enslaved Africans could find the freedom and capacity to participate in the divine act of constituting themselves; in remaking themselves with whatever resources they had at hand. "During sundown to sunup, enslaved African and African Americans, wrapped in the arms of the sacred, re-created themselves by seizing the initiative

> Necessity may be the mother of invention, but play is certainly the father.
> *Roger von Oech*
> *Contemporary American creativity guru*

in the crevices and pauses left vacant by the plantation system."[26] They found in these stolen moments and hidden spaces the opportunity to engage in a kind of playful reconstruction of their world. They converted a profane and secular time and space into divine time and space.

For enslaved Africans playing was not merely a diversion; it was a profoundly religious act. Hopkins argues that enslaved Africans fashioned a "theology of pleasure" in response to "the religious feel of and almost ultimate desire for fun times. . . . [T]he simple control of fun times in the theology of pleasure (that is, an area under sacred domain) marked one form of rebellion and re-created of the African American self."[27] Enslaved Africans found the freedom to re-create their religion and to refashion their relationship with nature. During sunup to sundown the enslaved African was seen as a part of nature to be conquered. During sundown to sunup enslaved Africans saw themselves as partners in communion with nature.

> Human beings need pleasure the way they need vitamins.
>
> *Lionel Tiger*
> *Contemporary Canadian anthropologist*

"[T]alking and walking in nature without the permission of the plantation authorities granted a true freedom and place for pleasure in the midst of their faith in a protective power greater than themselves."[28]

This period of play, or playing in the dark, was also often the occasion for the blossoming of romantic love. It was within the context of playing in the dark that one often searched for and found his or her soul mate. However, one of the most powerful examples of the ability of the enslaved African to play in the dark is "the corn shucking ritual." Seen from the perspective of the slave master, this practice of gathering enslaved Africans from surrounding plantations to peel the husks from the fall harvest was an efficient way of preparing the yield for the market. However, from the perspective of the enslaved African, it was an occasion for singing, laughing, dancing, and joking.

The corn shucking ritual occurred during the harvest season. Slave gangs from surrounding plantations would sing as they approached the particular plantation where a huge mountain of raw corn ears waited to be stripped of their outer skins. Upon arrival, two teams of workers were chosen, with either one or two "generals." After the designated signal, each general urged on his team, all hoping to be the first to finish shucking their section of the mountain of raw corn. The generals led their teams in song, laughter, and joking. After the pile had been sheared of the outer skins, all the slaves shared in a banquet. Then the master was hoisted up into the air and he and the mistress were made fun of by the black folk. Under the cover of frivolity, enslaved African Americans could say what they wanted about the master. Next came dancing and more singing. Finally, the various slave gangs returned to the roads as they sang their ways back home.[29]

Views diverge on whether this ritual was anything more than a carnival of clowns performing for the amusement of the slave master. However, by looking beneath the surface, we may discern a deeper, spiritual meaning in the act. It is a quintessential example of enslaved Africans *playing in the dark*. This ritual is the origin of the colloquial phrase *shuckin' and jivin'*, which means something akin to "playing around." It is important to note that this act of playing took place in the period when enslaved

Africans were about the business of reconstituting their lives and fortifying themselves for the terror of sunrise. Playing in the dark was an act of self-preservation.

Play within the community of enslaved Africans functioned in ways that were both similar and dissimilar to its function in other communities. Central ideas about play by several of the eminent thinkers in the first part of the twentieth century might be illuminating here. The emphasis on the relationship between play and the development of the self, as noted by Hopkins, was also an important component of the thought of the social psychologist George Herbert Mead. Mead argued that play is "a stage in the genesis of the self" in which persons learn social meanings and acquire a social language.[30]

The educational philosopher John Dewey argued that there is a difference between authentic free play and "fooling around." Dewey asserted that "'fooling, which was not necessarily 'foolishness,' occurred when an overflow of energy was temporarily disconnected from other acts. Fooling was 'fantastic, arbitrary, [and] aimless.'"[31] Dewey associated authentic play with the act of creation, especially as seen in art. Authentic play had the goal of creation, while fooling was "goalless." Part of the problem with Dewey's assertion—and we acknowledge that justice cannot be done to the complexity of his thought in this brief reflection—is that in the context of the enslavement of Africans as noted above, a facile and radical distinction between creative play and fooling around is not always helpful in ferreting out the true meaning and function of play.

Jane Addams, educational philosopher and activist, argued that play is a critical aspect of human educational development: "Culture is not mere learning, pegging away and getting a lot of things in one's head, but it means the power of enjoyment as one goes along, the power to play with a fact and get pleasure out of it."[32] The importance of Addams's insight is that under certain circumstances—and here I am arguing that the enslavement of Africans in America is an example of such circumstances—play itself could be the avenue to revelation. Through play, enslaved Africans learned about the nature of the reality in which they found themselves, as well as strategies for navigating that reality.

Those who play rarely become brittle in the face of stress or lose the healing capacity for humor.

Stuart Brown, MD
Contemporary American
psychiatrist

Slavery and Child's Play

As noted in chapter 1, the scope of this book does not include the substantial research on the play of children or animals. However, because in ways enslaved Africans were thought to be childlike, the play of the children of enslaved Africans may shed some light on the theme of play among African Americans in general. Bernard Mergen, in his helpful work *Play and Playthings*, devotes a chapter to the play of slave children.[33] Mergen notes that "one of the ironies of history is that far more is known about the play of slave children in the South than of free children in the North because of the Federal Writer's Project of the New Deal. The more than three thousand interviews with former slaves collected by the Writer's Project yield over three hundred individual descriptions of children's play in the slave states."[34] After a thorough discussion of the play of slave children, Mergen argues that a major obstacle in fully understanding the significance of the play of slave children is a reluctance to recognize the European origins of many of the play activities.

This is a perennial point of discussion among historians and certainly has validity. However, the point of play is that its creative function is tied not to who invented the game but to how the game is played. Mergen does observe that even when it appears that slave children learned games from their European counterparts, the slave children always felt free to alter, modify, and even transform those games as they saw fit. Mergen also notes that the play activities of slave children were shaped by the experience of slavery. One of the effects of slavery on the play of children was to, in many instances, make any "artificial distinctions between work, play, and ritual . . . unnecessary."[35] The play of children in slavery bore structural similarities and continuities with the play of adults in slavery.

Play in the slave community often seemed to be harmless frivolity at best, and downright foolish at worst. However, it appears that this act of playing has a much deeper meaning. As Brian Sutton-Smith observes, "Play's supposed frivolity may itself be a mask for play's use in more widespread systems for denigrating the play of other groups, as has been done characteristically throughout history by those of higher status against the recreations of those of lower status."[36] While much of the research on slavery, as well as the public perception of the meaning of slavery in our national consciousness, focuses on slavery as a source of unpaid labor, it may well be that an underappreciated contribution of enslaved Africans to the West is play that was creative, revolutionary, and liberating.

Zora Neale Hurston's *Their Eyes Were Watching God*

Zora Neale Hurston's profound narrative *Their Eyes Were Watching God* provides a significant opportunity to examine the meaning of play—specifically playing in the dark—as a literary theme. This is the story of Janie, who is raised by her grandmother, Nanny. Nanny has endured most of the indignities commonly associated with women sharing her lot. She has been physically, emotionally, sexually, and spiritually abused at the hands of her enslavers. The spirit of hope has been nearly obliterated in her. However, in the midst of this experience, she retains hope for a better life for her daughter. Her daughter is raped by a white schoolteacher and the product of that rape is Janie. Nanny's daughter, unable to come to terms with what has happened to her, leaves her daughter to be raised by Nanny. Nanny attempts to pass on the best wisdom that she has to her granddaughter, but that wisdom is weighted down with the pain of her past. In a particularly poignant and well-known scene, Nanny tells Janie, "Honey, de white man is de ruler of everything as fur as Ah been able tuh find out . . . de white man throw down de load and tell the nigger man tuh pick it up. He pick it up because he have to, but he don't tote it. He hand it to his womenfolks. De nigger woman is de mule uh de world so fur as Ah can see."

> In every real man a child is hidden that wants to play.
>
> *Friedrich Nietzsche*
> *German philosopher*
> *1844-1900*

This section of dialogue has been the starting point of much of the critical commentary on this novel. Indeed, the experience described by Nanny has been thought to speak to the experience not only of African American women but, by extension, of all women. As such, it has become a feminist text in the eyes of many. Whether or not reading this text as a feminist text is warranted given the unique and specific experiences explored therein might be a fruitful line of inquiry. However, for the purposes of this chapter, we want to turn our attention in another direction.

The first half of the novel treats the slow decline of hope and optimism in Janie. Both of her marriages are casualties not just of the irresistible forces of oppression and Jim Crow but of an inability on the part of her husbands to find the resources necessary to give and preserve life for Janie. Her first husband, Logan Killicks, is a much older man who has amassed some property. When Janie declares that she does not want Logan Killicks, Nanny replies, " 'Taint Logan Killicks Ah wants you to have, baby, it's protection."[37] Nanny is concerned that Janie may be left destitute after her death, and Killicks represents security. He may have been "a good man" as her grandmother said, but Janie discovers after marrying him that "marriage did not make love." Thus, her "first dream [of romance] was dead, so she became a woman."[38] Nanny's observation of the place of black women in the world almost becomes a prediction as Killicks, in a final bid to break Janie's will, informs her that he is going to see a man about buying a mule. Knowing that he already has a mule, Janie questions him about the need for a second one. Killicks simply says that potatoes are going to be the big crop this year and that the mule he is purchasing has been "all gentled up so even uh woman kin handle 'im."[39] Janie, unwilling to become a mule by walking behind one, runs away to Joe Starks, an ambitious man and her second husband.

Joe Starks is a dramatic contrast to Killicks. He is upwardly mobile and painfully aware of his social status. He is determined to put Janie on a pedestal. He keeps her more as a symbol of his achievement than as a wife and partner. While Killicks wanted to work her to death, Starks is determined to shield her from the rough-and-tumble world of commerce and social exchange. In particular, as the men gathered at the end of the day in front of the store owned by Starks, Janie was expressly forbidden from participating in the jovial storytelling and verbal jousting that provided release from backbreaking and poorly compensated labor. It was on one occasion that Janie took part in the game known as "playing the dozens," an exchange of good-natured but semi-serious insults. Janie more than holds her own with the men gathered there, and after a victorious round, Joe Starks takes exception to this display of strength and independence on the part of his wife, "so he struck Janie with all of his might and drove her from the store."[40] Joe Starks dies from a kidney ailment, but his spirit was already a casualty of his empty pursuit of status. One could sum up the first half of the novel as follows: Janie is stifled by one husband who believed that a woman is meant to work and should have no time to play, and another husband who believed that a woman should have no business playing.

The second half of the novel describes Janie's relationship with Vergible "Tea Cake" Woods. Tea Cake is unlike any other man Janie has ever met. He is polite, confident, self-possessed, and definitely interested in her. The attraction is mutual, even though Janie is older than he. But almost immediately, Tea Cake begins to change Janie's perspective on life by introducing or reintroducing her to the idea of play. In an early encounter, Tea Cake invites

Janie to a game of checkers. Janie notes that while the game is treasured among the men of the area, she never learned—or was never allowed to learn—to play. Tea Cake took the checkerboard, "set it up and began to show her and she found herself glowing inside. Somebody wanted her to play. Somebody thought it natural for her to play."[41] The game that follows is not so much competition as it is co-creation, not so much instruction as it is discovery.

> Play allows us to develop alternatives to violence and despair; it helps us learn perseverance and gain optimism.
>
> Stuart Brown, MD
> Contemporary American psychiatrist

Early in the description of their relationship, it is during the night that a significant portion of her self-discovery takes place. On a whim, Tea Cake takes Janie fishing. "It was so crazy digging worms by lamp light and setting out for Lake Sabelia after midnight that she felt like a child breaking rules. That's what made Janie like it. They caught two or three and got home just before day."[42] In a particularly revealing moment, Tea Cake, who works during the day, takes off from work to see Janie in the daytime. This is important because he wants her to know that what she experiences with him at night is consistent with who he is in the daytime. "Thought Ah'd try tuh git heah soon enough tuh tell yuh may daytime thoughts. Ah see yuh needs tuh know mah daytime feelings. Ah can't sense yuh intuh it at night."[43] Janie's life is being completely redefined. "Tea Cake and Janie gone hunting. Tea Cake and Janie gone fishing. Tea Cake and Janie gone to Orlando to the movies. Tea Cake and Janie gone to a dance . . . Tea Cake and

Janie playing checkers; playing coon-can; playing Florida flip on the store porch all afternoon as if nobody else was there. Day after day and week after week."[44]

These playful activities are even the basis of the criticism she receives from one of the women of the community who believes that she is living beneath her status as the widow of Joe Starks. "Janie, everybody's talkin' 'bout how dat Tea Cake is draggin' you round tuh places you ain't used tuh. Baseball games and huntin' and fishin'. He don't know you'se useter uh more high time crowd than dat. You always did class off."[45] One of the themes of the novel is that this playful activity was something engaged in only by the lower-class folk in the community. On one occasion a woman who is a mulatto and therefore considers herself— and Janie—to be of a higher class than other black folk, disparages play, associating it with unadulterated blackness. "[Black folk] makes me tired. Always laughin'! Dey laughs too much and dey laughs too loud. Always singin' ol' nigger songs! Always cuttin' de monkey for white folks. If it wuzn't for so many black folks it wouldn't be no race problem. De white folks would take us in wid dem. De black ones is holdin' us back."[46] But this kind of play is not merely amusement; it is part of life and love itself. It is connected with romance. Janie notes that she married Tea Cake for reasons of the heart alone. Unlike her previous marriages, "dis ain't no business proposition, and no race after property and titles. Dis is uh love game."[47]

During their marriage Janie makes a fundamental discovery about Tea Cake. Tea Cake takes some money that belongs to Janie and spends it engaging in a side of him that he wants to keep secret from Janie. He gambles, fights, wins and loses. He enjoys life to the fullest but does it without his wife because he does not want her to see "the commonness" in him. After returning home he describes his adventure to Janie, and she insists that whatever he is involved in she wants to be involved in. Reassured by her words, Tea Cake vows to win her money back. When Janie asks how he will do this, Tea Cake responds, "Honey, since you loose me and gimme privilege tuh tell yuh all about mahself, Ah'll tell yuh. You done married one uh de best gamblers God ever made. Cards or dice either one."[48] When Tea Cake hears about a game taking place nearby, he leaves to win back the money. This game—this nocturnal contest—has its dangers. Tea Cake wins the money but is cut in the aftermath. There are dangers to playing in the dark. Yet those dangers are counted as part of the game.

Tea Cake is not only interested in Janie as a play partner. He does not divide life into distinct categories of work and play. This is evident in his invitation to Janie to come with him to "the muck"—that is, the Everglades—where fertile soil draws souls searching for the resources for a better life. The muck is not just the place "where dey raise all dat cane and stringbeans and tomatuhs. Folks don't do nothin' down dere but make money and fun and foolishness."[49] Tea Cake says, "All day Ah'm pickin' beans. All night Ah'm pickin' mah box and rollin' dice. Between de beans and de dice Ah can't lose."[50] But Tea Cake does not exclude Janie from any aspect of his life. He invites Janie to come to the fields and work with him.

Unlike Killicks, who wanted to work her to death because that was all she was good for, or Starks, who did not want her to work because he thought she was useless, Tea Cake is simply in love with Janie and cannot bear to be away from her. She happily agrees, although "it was generally assumed that she thought herself too good to work like the rest of the women and that Tea Cake 'pomped her up tuh dat.' But all day long the romping and playing they carried on behind the boss's back made her popular right away. It got the whole field to playing off and on. Then Tea Cake would help her get supper afterwards."[51] Janie played, gambled, won, and lost. She also rediscovered her voice and was encouraged to tell stories again. "She got so she could tell big stories herself from listening to the rest."[52] Sherley Anne Williams in her excellent introduction to the novel comments on this theme: "Tea Cake asks and Janie consents to work in the fields with him, because neither wants to be parted from the other even during the work day. Their love for each other makes the stoop labor of bean picking seem almost play."[53]

> Children have always learned and created places for themselves through play.
>
> *Donna R. Barnes*
> *Contemporary American psychologist*

The novel ends tragically with the death of Tea Cake by Janie's hand after he was bitten by a rabid dog during a hurricane. Yet this theme of play, and playing in the dark, sheds some light on the passage from which the novel gets its title. In the middle of the hurricane, as Janie and Tea Cake attempt to ride out the storm, "the wind came back with triple fury, and put out the light for the last time. They sat in company with the others in other shanties, their eyes straining against crude walls and their souls asking if He meant to measure their puny might against His. They seemed to be staring at the dark, but their eyes were watching God."[54]

God and Playing in the Dark

Playing in the dark is not an act of despair or hopeless-ness. It is the process through which divine self-revelation takes place. The purpose of play is creative. This creative activity has three dimensions as uncovered by this analysis of play. First, play is connected to romantic love. The ability to play with one's lover is a powerful theme in biblical faith. The Song of Songs, commonly understood as an allegory for God's love for humanity and Christ's love for the church, is an example of the play between lovers.

Second, play is connected with storytelling. The creation narratives of Genesis were the result of the need to tell the story of human existence in a celebratory fashion. Genesis asserts that God faced a great void or darkness and in response to it not only spoke light into being but engaged in the creation of all that is. In the opening chapter of the Gospel of John, the writer declares that God was present in the darkness but that God and the light of God were not overcome by that darkness.

Third, play is connected with hope. Hope is the recognition that the way in which the future will unfold is not given to us to know—even if it is known by God. In hope we are allowed to play with the possibilities that life presents to us and to imagine new worlds.

The darkness into which Tea Cake and Janie stared is the same darkness on which Toni Morrison opines. It may be the darkness of Plato's cave against which a critical epistemology emerged. This is the darkness against which enslaved Africans played their games of survival and wholeness. At this point we turn our attention to what these reflections might say to our understanding of God.

These reflections on play suggest fresh ways to think about God in Christian traditions. Central to Christian affirmations about God is that God is creator, redeemer, and sustainer. These symbolic expressions, especially that God is creator and redeemer, may provide the language for talking about God in light of our observations on play.

One might think of God as the architect of the field of play. Christian thought has traditionally affirmed God as creator of the world. One point of contention among Christian thinkers has been the character of that world. That is, is that world a place from which we long to escape because it is evil, or is that world a place that continually and without contradiction manifests the goodness of God? These are the extremes, for most Christians, I would argue, see the world as neither fundamentally evil—for that would mean that something that God has created has gone completely awry—nor completely benevolent—for that would mean that the world has a character that belongs only to its creator. Most Christians would say that the world is deeply flawed while remaining a creation of God or that the world manifests the image of its creator, though it is deeply distorted.

Our reflections on play suggest that if the world is a field of play, then God might be understood as its architect. This field might be understood as having a uniformity, a consistent gestalt, much like a regulation basketball court whose dimensions never change. Yet within that uniformity, as the exploits of Bob Cousy, Magic Johnson, Julius Erving, and Michael Jordan have demonstrated, true creativity continually takes place.

On the other hand, this field might be understood as having variety, or a contextual identity, much like great golf courses, each of which is unique; so much so that the course becomes part of the play activity itself.

Yet champion golfers—from Byron Nelson to Charlie Sifford to Arnold Palmer to Nancy Lopez to Jack Nicklaus to Eldrick "Tiger" Woods—have demonstrated that innate and consistent ability to play well on a variety of "fields."[55]

The field of play, or "the mission field" for the early church, was more than the strict architectonic, culturally bounded field of traditional Judaism. Nor was it the ever-changing, eclectic, chameleon-like field of infinite religious pluralism of the early Roman Empire (they even had a statue devoted to "the unknown God"). Within the cultural and religious complexity of the listeners at Pentecost, boundaries—new, expanded boundaries for the Jews, yet still boundaries for the Greeks—were revealed for this divine field of play.

> There is for many a poverty of play.
>
> D. W. Winnicott
> British pediatrician
> 1896–1971

Another point of contention in Christian thinking about the world has been its telos, or its destiny. Is the world substantially outside of any context of preexistent time—or cosmological history—making the time between the beginning of the world and the end of the world the only meaningful time, or is the world essentially part of the general flow of time, rendering the earthly duration of time a minute occurrence within that flow?

Again, these are extremes, for to assert that the time between the beginning and end of the world is the only meaningful time would be to make God captive to time as we experience it. Likewise, to assert that there is nothing special about the time that has been given to us would miss its potential to unfold in a progressive manner. In fact, the center of Christian affirmation about the temporal context of the world declares that the world exists in general time and history bounded by an opportunistic purpose (eternal), or that the world exists in a specific time and history imbued with purposeful opportunity (teleological). It is this sense of opportunity and purpose that constitutes the redemptive activity of God in the world.

Our reflections on play suggest not only that the world is a field of play but that the temporal context of the world is "playtime." God is not only the architect of the field of play but also the time-keeper. In one sense, play is conscribed by time. In most venues the time of play is set, usually by a clock. All play activity must take place between two temporal points, the beginning and the end. Yet even within the limits of clock-based play, creativity as opportunity is possible. Attentive players are able to manipulate time. By "working the clock," they can extend play and realize additional opportunities.

In another sense, play can take place outside the context of time. Here one might think of baseball, chess, or golf (especially in its purest match play format). Here time is bracketed for the purpose of play.[56] (In golf there is the issue of the speed of play, but this is more of an economic issue than one directly connected with the play itself.) But the fact is that no play activity can be permanently bracketed from the flow of time and history. Urgency is added to golf by limiting the number of holes in stroke play, and the number of innings in baseball give the activity a sense of purpose. While opportunity may appear to be extended, play will eventually end.

Underneath the notion that time has a predictable endpoint is not simply a millennialist sternness and the conviction of a coming apocalypse. Underneath this notion is the idea of purpose. Underneath the notion that there is always time is not simply a pursuit of leisure and an assumption of immortality. Underneath this notion is the idea of opportunity.

For the early church, play time, or "the day of the Lord," was limited neither by the expectation of a Jewish Messiah with its apocalyptic mindset nor by the fatalistic chronology of the Greco-Roman mindset that said, "Let us eat, drink, and be merry for tomorrow we die." The day of the Lord, or play time, was framed by what Paul Tillich called "kairos," moments of both purpose and opportunity. Even the delayed parousia did not destroy the historical consciousness or sense of temporal urgency for the early church but affirmed that even time itself was in God's hands. The purpose in time is evident in the verse "God desires that none be lost." The opportunity in time is evident in the verse "You know not the day or hour."

God's creative activity is evident in the divine design of a field of play. And for those who feel that they have no place to play, the world is a "field of dreams." God's redemptive activity is evident in the designation of a time for play. For those who feel that the time for them to play has expired, history is the story of overtime. It is the continual interaction of creation—the field of play—and redemption—the time of play—that constitutes God's sustaining activity.

The early church played in dark places, not just the catacombs and caves of subterranean sanctuaries but also within the darkened consciousness of people who sought a new place. The early church played within dark times, not just during the periods of subjugation and corruption by an external foe but also within the dim desperation of people who sought a new day.

In similar fashion, as we have seen, black folk in their search for meaning and wholeness were not afraid to play in the dark, casting their lot with God. Perhaps it is by learning again to play in the dark that we might not only see the light but recognize that light as God.

3

don't hate the player, hate the game: jesus as a player

And David said unto Michal, It was before the LORD, which chose me before thy father, and before all his house, to appoint me ruler over the people of the LORD, over Israel: therefore will I play before the LORD.

2 Samuel 6:21

Play is a quintessential human activity. It is something we do not only as children but also as we go through the life cycle. Play has acquired a variety of meanings and connotations. In chapter 1 we briefly reviewed some of the major themes and motifs in play theory and research. We have seen that play has been a key concept in philosophy, sociology, psychology, literary studies, and even theology. Play is also a fluid concept. In addition to the more obvious and familiar connotations of the term, play has acquired a meaning within popular culture, and especially within African American culture, that goes beyond mere frivolity.

The phrase serving as the title for this chapter is grounded in this deeper meaning. "Don't hate the player, hate the game" is in one sense derived from the quasi-biblical saying "Don't hate the sinner, hate the sin."

This phrase, used in various urban, African American–influenced cultural settings, has a distinctive meaning. The "player" in this context is often a street hustler, a con man, or even (in the past) a pimp. The player can also be a person who lives the lifestyle of a gambler. In this context, the player is one known to engage in high stakes games and to embrace risk. More obviously, the player is one who excels in some athletic contest. However, what makes the player unique is a particular personal gift or charism. Whether the field of play is the street, the casino, or the basketball court, the player is a person who has developed the capacity to navigate complex social, cultural, and religious systems and to survive them. What makes the player such a fascinating character is that these systems are often not designed to benefit the player. In fact, the systems are generally hostile to the player. The player consciously lives within those systems but does not accommodate them. The player is sometimes a rebel but not necessarily a revolutionary.

> Play, while it cannot change the external realities of children's lives, can be a vehicle for children to explore and enjoy their differences and similarities and to create, even for a brief time, a more just world where everyone is an equal and valued participant.
>
> *Patricia G. Ramsey*
> *Contemporary American*
> *educational psychologist*

The purpose of this chapter is to explore this notion of the player and the game with some attention to its deeper dimensions. That is, play as a fundamentally human activity has a political, social, and religious meaning. While it is impossible to separate these dimensions of play completely (nor would we want to impoverish our analysis by attempting to do so), our primary focus will be on the religious and theological dimensions of this concept. In chapter 2 we treated the notion of play and its relationship to our understanding of God. In this chapter we will examine the notion of play as it relates to the quintessential God-man, Jesus the Christ. In essence, we will ask what the idea behind the phrase "don't hate the player, hate the game" has to do with our theological understanding of Jesus Christ.

Play and the Bible

Play is an important, if not central, theme in the Bible. However, somber cultural influences, especially those of the Puritans, have made it difficult to appreciate play in the Bible. The scriptural passage that serves as an epigraph to this chapter sheds some light on the meaning of play in the Bible. The sixth chapter of 2 Samuel contains the account of David's joyous and triumphant return to Jerusalem with the Ark of the Covenant. David's unrestrained jubilation is symbolized by his complete disregard for decorum. He dances with all his might and he dances right out of his clothes. His wife Michal, who observes David's exhibition, finds it odious. David, however, will not have his joy tempered and declares that he will continue to "play before

> A child who does not play is not a child, but the man who does not play has lost forever the child who lived in him.
>
> *Pablo Neruda*
> *Chilean poet*
> *1904–1973*

the Lord." In this story, David is the player, and Michal is the player hater.

Play often tends to elicit one of two responses in people. Either they join the play and affirm its validity, or they reject the play and pronounce it inappropriate or foolish. However, it is usually not the play that is expressly hated but the player. In this story David engages in what I call a royal type of play. The form of David's play, while in Michal's eyes unbefitting of a king, is precisely the kind of play in which a king can engage. Roger Callois posits a distinction between two types of play. The first is "paidia, which is active, tumultous, exuberant, and spontaneous." The second is "ludus, representing calculation, contrivance, and subordination to rules."[1] David's celebration is an example of this first type of play. It is related to the play of a child. One can imagine David whirling about until, disheveled and giddy, he falls into the Palestinian dust overcome by joy.

When one thinks of the biblical picture of Jesus, one would be hard pressed to find a similar example of Jesus in the midst of unrestrained jubilation. Indeed, most depictions of Jesus portray him as one who took life too seriously to engage in such frivolity. However, it is my contention that Jesus also engaged in a kind of play. Jesus' play, unlike David's royal play, is the play of the common person. Jesus' play is ludic according to Callois's definition. It is calculation, contrivance, and the subordination *of* the rules. (While Callois speaks of subordination to rules, I argue that subordination to the rules is reached through a complex of practices that requires first a subordination of the rules. We can see this in Jesus' complex relationship to the legal practices and principles of his time.) We will return to a fuller examination of the notion of Jesus as a player later.

Play and the Person of Christ

In his book *Dionysus Reborn*, Mihai Spariosu makes an observation about the role of play in the development of Western philosophical discourse. "Another play concept that reflects the shift from a prerational to a rational mentality in Hellenic thought is that of play as an *as if* activity or mode of being. This concept is related both to mimesis-play and to mimesis-imitation through the idea of *homoiosis* (likeness)."[2] The term *homoiosis* has a long history in theological discourse about the identity (and work) of Jesus Christ.[3] In fact, the first ecumenical council held in Nicaea in 325 C.E. was convened to determine whether orthodox belief would affirm that Jesus Christ was of the same substance as God the Father or of similar substance (*homoiosis*).

As astronauts and space travelers children puzzle over the future; as dinosaurs and princesses they unearth the past. As weather reporters and restaurant workers they make sense of reality; as monsters and gremlins they make sense of the unreal.

Gretchen Owocki
Contemporary American
early childhood educator

The result of the council was that the orthodox position substantially identified Jesus and God the Father. From that point on, to assert that their relationship was one of "likeness" was heresy. There was no room for any play between the person of Jesus and the being of God. However, Arius, the protagonist of the council of Nicaea, held a position equally uncomfortable with the idea of play in Christological affirmations. Arius's error was not that he eliminated the notion of play but that he proposed to resolve it in the wrong way. By claiming that Jesus was created by God, and therefore was not God, Arius simply sought to remove the play in Christ to the left rather than to the right.

In every subsequent major Christological controversy, play as that *set of activities or practices or ideas that occurs in the interstices between freedom and structure, between the subject(ive) and object(ive), between creation and imitation* is a contributing factor. The *docetic* claim that Jesus never really suffered but only appeared to suffer because he was not really human was rejected because it took the play out of the understanding of Jesus Christ. On the other hand, the *adoptionist* claim that Jesus was the son of God by virtue of his adoption by God and was therefore in essence only human was rejected because it took the play out of the understanding of Jesus Christ. Play occurs in the interstices. Tertullian's defense of the incarnation as a dynamic unity of the humanity and the divinity of Christ, and Origen's claim that Christ represented a "mediator" between God and humanity, preserves this element of play.

So, in all these spheres—in painting, sculpture, drawing, music, singing, dancing, gymnastics, games, sports, writing and speech—we can carry on to our heart's content, all through our long lives, complex and specialized forms of exploration and experiment.

Desmond Morris
Contemporary British
zoologist

Even G. E. Lessing's famous declaration that there is "an ugly ditch" between "the accidental truths of history" and "the necessary truths of reason" when it comes to knowing who and what Jesus Christ is depends on a positive valuation of the play between the two.[4] It is the play between what we do know about Jesus and what we can know about Christ that funds the dynamic of Christology. It is an uneasiness with the play between apparently competing claims that gives rise to heresies.

Peter Berger, in his work *The Heretical Imperative*, notes that the word *heresy* is derived from the Greek word *hairesis*, which means "the act of choosing."[5] The heretical imperative is the demand to choose one of two apparently contradictory claims rather than let them play with one another. The fact is that heresy, whether it is Pelagianism or Donatism, is anti-play. Heresy renders play impossible. To summarize, the perennial questions about the person of Jesus Christ and their resolution suggest that, in the eyes of the ancient councils, play between competing claims is central to the person of Jesus Christ.

Jaroslav Pelikan, in his suggestive work *Jesus through the Centuries*, identifies and discusses a myriad of images of Jesus from around the world.[6] Jesus is seen as the Rabbi, the Light of the Gentiles, the King of Kings, the Cosmic Christ, the Monk Who Rules the World, the Prince of Peace, the Poet of the Spirit, and the Liberator, among others. These images play with and among themselves, eliciting new meanings and older insights. These images of Jesus speak to the reality that our ideas of Jesus are variable. This is what makes them culturally relevant. However, the reason that these images and others are recognizable as images of Jesus is that they share some structural relationship. This is what makes them theologically true.

Similarly, Brian Sutton-Smith describes play as embodying both "adaptive variability" and "structural similarity."[7] That is, play can and does appear across history in an almost endless variety of forms, yet it is always recognizable in every epoch as play. Play is central to who Jesus is because he appears in a variety of cultural and historical images but is always recognizable theologically and devotionally as Jesus of Nazareth. This is why attempts to establish definitively who Jesus was and what he actually said, apart from the diverse imagination of the first and subsequent Christian communities, fall flat. It is impossible to take the play out of Jesus Christ. He does and will continue to play across the collective consciousness of Christian communities.

Play and the Saving Activity of Jesus

Play is important in understanding not only the person of Jesus Christ but also the activity of Jesus Christ. Much theological discussion about Jesus Christ focuses on his work of atonement and redemption. It is my contention that even using the term *work* to describe this activity obscures one of its basic features. Here we are focused on a submerged and neglected aspect of Jesus' activity—play. Classical and traditional statements of the atonement/redemption activity of Jesus Christ are funded in

> We all need empty hours in our lives or we will have no time to create or dream.
>
> Robert Coles
> Contemporary American
> child psychologist

part by this notion of play. Irenaeus's ransom theory of the atonement claims that humanity had to be purchased from Satan at the price of the life of Christ. Here, human beings can be seen as pawns—albeit valuable pawns—in a grand game between God and Satan. Irenaeus also develops the notion of the atonement as "recapitulation." Brian Sutton-Smith describes play as recapitulation, as a reenactment or re-creation in which some primal balance is restored. This same emphasis is present in Irenaeus's work.

> The debt we owe to the play of the imagination is incalculable.
>
> *Carl Jung*
> *Swiss psychoanalyst*
> *1875–1961*

One of the most interesting theories of the atonement is the "mousetrap" theory developed by Rufinus of Aquileia. In this theory, the purpose of the incarnation was to provide bait with which to hook Satan. Here God and Satan are engaged in a no-holds-barred contest, and Jesus is in play. Anselm of Canterbury's theory of satisfaction claims that through sin God was dishonored. This honor must be restored through some satisfaction. Only Jesus Christ is capable of satisfying that loss. Certainly in feudal societies, honor and shame formed the context of a game in which Jesus Christ was the central player.

Even Gustaf Aulen's classic theory of the atonement asserts that the atonement is best understood as a drama in which Christ is the central player. The atonement, in this view, is in essence a play. While traditionally the atonement and redemption wrought by Jesus Christ are referred to as "work," they are also, if not primarily, play. In the soteriological examples noted above, it is Jesus

Christ as the Son of God who is the major player in the redemptive drama.

The major critique of most soteriological theories is that they are based on circumstances that in themselves are morally objectionable. Why does God's injured honor require the sacrifice of Christ? Why must an omnipotent God set a trap for the devil? These are games, and Jesus Christ is a player in them. However, in all of these examples, faith requires that one reserve one's odium for the existence of evil and suffering. That is, one should not hate the player but hate the game.

The soteriological activity of Jesus Christ is not limited to the heavenly game contested between God and the power of sin and evil. The saving activity of Jesus Christ also occurs in the earthly game contested at the levels of culture, politics, and religion. It is to the issue of Jesus Christ as a player in this earthly game that we now turn our attention. There is a common feature at the heart of our understanding of Jesus Christ and what some scholars have observed about the nature of play. "The single most important and widely agreed-upon structural thesis brought forward about play in the twentieth century is . . . that play is a kind of paradox. [This] means that play always is and is not what it displays itself to be."[8] Jesus Christ is the great paradox at the heart of Christianity. He always is and is not what he appears to be. It is with this insight in mind that we posit, in a preliminary way, three dimensions of Jesus Christ as player.

Jesus as a Cultural Player

Recent scholarship has identified the cultural context in which Jesus lived as one dominated by an honor/shame matrix.[9] Honor was the social currency that separated the cultural haves from the cultural have-nots. David A. deSilva notes:

> Honor is a dynamic and relational concept. On the one hand, an individual can think of himself or herself as honorable based on his or her conviction that he or she has embodied those actions and qualities that the group values as "honorable," as the marks of a valuable person. This aspect of honor is really "self-respect." on the other hand, honor is also the esteem in which a person is held by the person's group that he or she is a valuable member of that group. In this regard, it is having the respect of others. It was a problematic experience when one's self-respect was not matched by corresponding respect from others, but strategies could be developed to cope with discrepancy here. When the powerful and the masses, the philosophers and the Jews, the pagans and the Christians all regarded honor and dishonor as their primary axis of value, each group would fill out the picture of what constituted honorable behavior or character in terms of its own distinctive sets of beliefs and values, and

Ritual grew up in sacred play; poetry was born in play and nourished on play; music and dancing were pure play. . . . We have to conclude, therefore, that civilization is, in its earliest phases, played. It does not come from play . . . it arises in and as play, and never leaves it.

Johan Huizinga
Dutch historian
1872–1945

would evaluate people both inside and outside that group accordingly.[10]

This honor and shame system actually functioned as a game in which there were winners and losers. One could be a winner by claiming honor through precedence—achieving social status, power, and prestige. Or one could attain honor through competition in sports or otherwise.

Honor in this context was reserved for free men. Slaves, women, and peasants could never hope to attain such honor but only to avoid shame. However, their status as slaves, women, and peasants meant that shame was ever present in their lives. It was into this honor and shame game that Jesus appeared as a player par excellence. Here Jesus is a player because play, in this sense, is a means to survival. Play is "contemplative decision making in thoughts and actions . . . associated with attempts to secure survival through careful delays and reconsiderations."[11] Jesus' primary audience as a cultural player was that group of people who were the grand losers in the honor and shame game. These were not people for whom leisure was a significant part of life. Civil rights leader Ralph Abernathy comments on the relationship between poor people and leisure: "It is a misnomer to think that poor people have leisure time. Their total existence is for survival. . . . While poor people do have their moments of escape from the reality of being poor,

> I believe that those boys who take part in rough, hard play outside of school will not find any need for horse-play in school.
>
> *Theodore Roosevelt*
> *American president*
> *1858–1919*

their escape pattern usually turns toward the continuous attempt to break out of the trap of despairing poverty. . . . There is no leisure time for poor people. . . . Many poor escape this kind of existence for whatever solace can be found in the whiskey bottle and in hard drugs. But they know—all of us know—that is not leisure."[12]

Jesus' interaction was with the peasant class of his day who were struggling for survival and for whom leisure was an unaffordable luxury. However, Jesus could, as a player par excellence, teach them how to play the game. Jesus' primary approach was to show his listeners how "through careful delays and reconsiderations" to manage their way through daily life. He reminded his followers that "the stone that the builders rejected has become the cornerstone" (Mark 12:10-11). He reminded his followers that "the Son of Man came not to be served but to serve" (Mark 10:45). He reminded his followers that "the last shall be first and the first shall be last" (Luke 13:30).

As a cultural player Jesus was able to navigate the cultural honor/shame system by including the shamed and the dishonored in the game, and by introducing grace as a modifier of the game.[13] He brought grace to the game. Through grace as surplus and forgiveness, Jesus was able to impute honor to the dishonored. One of the grand, if overlooked, features of the civil rights movement of the mid-twentieth century was the emergence of a people who were deemed to be among the shamed and their insistent demand for the honor that was due them. In their dress, demeanor, words, and walk, those who participated in the marches and boycotts claimed a place of honor. They modeled their behavior on that of Jesus. By his example and instruction, he was able to show them how to play and survive the game.

Jesus as a Political Player

Jesus was not only a player in his cultural setting; he was also a player in his political setting. While the biblical narratives recount his encounters with political power from the moment of his conception to the moment of his death and beyond, the full understanding of the significance of these encounters can be advanced by looking at Jesus' activity as a player.

Research on play has emphasized the development of mastery by the player. Jean Piaget, an expert on child development, developed a theory of "mastery play." This mastery is achieved through "the crucial processes of assimilation and accommodation—by modifying the world to [one's] own notions and by changing [one's] actions to suit the world's demands."[14] Piaget's definition of mastery play as involving assimilation and accommodation has been critiqued and modified by recent thinkers. One of the more creative modifications has been to distinguish between *play* and *flow*. "In play, skills exceed challenge, but in flow . . . they are matched."[15] Piaget's focus on play as assimilation and accommodation suggests that play is primarily associated with survival rather than mastery. In this definition, play is mastery because skills exceed challenge.

Jesus was a political player precisely because he was able to master his political environment. The church's claim that Jesus was victorious over his political environment was, in this sense, more than just a theological

> Play is hard to maintain as you get older. You get less playful. You shouldn't, of course.
>
> *Richard Feynman*
> *American physicist*
> *1918–1988*

affirmation but in some important ways also a political fact. Jesus' mastery was mastery because he was able to move through and around the political authorities by redefining and segregating the field of play. This is what Jesus was doing when he responded to those who challenged his allegiance to imperial power by saying, "Render unto Caesar that which is Caesar's and unto God that which is God's" (Matthew 22:21). Jesus' claim to the title "Lord and Savior" was disputed because this title was also claimed by the emperor of Rome.

The essence of Jesus' identity as a political player is evident in his encounter with Pontius Pilate. That encounter is centered on Jesus' proclamation, "My kingdom is not from this world" (John 18:36). In this statement, Jesus seizes the opportunity to master his political environment. At this moment Jesus creatively and imaginatively engages Roman imperial power. He does so through mastery rather than conquest, freedom rather than force. J. C. Friedrich von Schiller, in his book *On the Aesthetic Education of Man*, observes that "in the midst of the awful realm of powers, and of the sacred realm of laws, the aesthetic creative impulse is building unawares a third joyous realm of play and appearance, in which it releases mankind from all the shackles of circumstance and frees him from everything that may be called constraint, whether physical or moral. . . . *To grant freedom by means of freedom* is the fundamental law of this kingdom.[16]

It is this freedom that enables the political player to play. It is not a freedom that is seized by the player rather

> The opposite of play is not work. It's depression.
>
> *Brian Sutton-Smith*
> *Contemporary American folklorist*

than given to her or him. William A. Sadler Jr. says that "in play an individual takes advantage of an opportunity to intensify and personalize his perception, to set the boundaries of his world, to forge an original space-time, a personal world. . . . In play, one constructs his own space, providing himself with a field of freedom in which to experiment with meanings and to establish his identity."[17]

Jesus, in his dealing with imperial power, is a player because he has the capacity to create and embody an alternative world. It is contrasted with the world of Roman imperial power. Jesus' kingdom is not of this world. John Dominic Crossan, in his book *God and Empire*, advises that we read this saying of Jesus in its fuller context.[18] The fuller context includes Jesus' affirmation that his disciples would not resort to violence even to save him from death. The difference between the kingdom that Jesus describes and that of Roman imperial power is that the former is one sustained by nonviolence while the latter is ruled by violence. This is why the appellation of revolutionary does not exhaust or capture the work of Jesus in his political context. Attempts to define him as a revolutionary have often required a restricted view of activity among us or a redefinition of the *revolution*. As a player, Jesus is able to master the political authorities of his day without confronting them directly. He is able to define a realm of political creativity and freedom in a politically repressive environment.

Malcolm X, an African American leader, was an example of a political player. He had the skills to maneuver his way through the political minefield of 1960s America. Simply by asserting the existence of a realm of freedom and creativity in which African Americans could express themselves, and by asserting that the creation of this realm would not be deterred by threats of violent repression by imperial power, he was called a separatist and an advocate of violence. It is highly likely that he simply employed the player skills that he acquired in the streets of Boston and New York to play the political game. The model for this kind of play is Jesus, who dared in the midst of Roman imperial power to propose and live according to another kingdom.

Jesus as a Religious Player

The social system of honor and shame provided the cultural field of play for Jesus, and the imperial power Rome provided the political field of play for Jesus. We turn now to Jesus as a religious player. The religious field of play for Jesus was that complex and seemingly ever-expanding constellation of laws and mandates that constituted Judaism in his day. This religious field was basic because it often undergirded the cultural field of honor and shame. And it was often either apathetic to or in collusion with the political field of imperial power. Jesus as a player engaged this religious field of play at three critical points: the meaning of the sabbath, the meaning of freedom, and the meaning of the future.

> The very existence of youth is due in part to the necessity for play; the animal does not play because he is young, he has a period of youth because he must play.
>
> *Karl Groos*
> *German evolutionary biologist*
> *1861–1946*

Each of the four Gospels describes an encounter between Jesus and his religious adversaries over the meaning of the sabbath.[19] In each case Jesus is accused of failing to observe the sabbath because he attends to human need during this sacred time. Jesus feeds his disciples and heals those who are wounded. When he is accused of violating the law, he points out that his adversaries have no problem saving their animals on the sabbath. Here Jesus reverses the valuation of animals or property over humans. He claims mastery over this moment by declaring that as the Son of Man he is the Lord of the sabbath.

In Jesus' time religious observance had become mere acquiescence to a set of rules whose logic and meaning had been distorted or obscured. Jesus as a player brought something different to this setting. Robert K. Johnston notes that "the player is someone who chooses a set of rules, an order, as a vehicle for the free expression of his or her joy, power, and spontaneity. The rules are important not for their own sake but for the sake of the play activity itself."[20] This was the essence of Jesus' approach to the law, especially as it related to the meaning of the sabbath. The sabbath had become important for its own sake rather for the sake of the joy and spontaneity of religious adoration. When Jesus declared himself Lord of the sabbath, he was claiming the law as a vehicle of devotion.

> Creative people are curious, flexible, persistent, and independent with a tremendous spirit of adventure and a love of play.
>
> *Henri Matisse*
> *French painter*
> *1869–1954*

One of the major features of play is freedom. Without freedom there is no possibility of play. Brazilian educator and theologian Rubem A. Alves observes that "play . . . creates an order out of imagination and therefore out of freedom"[21] Jesus was a player precisely because he was able to create order out of freedom. The freedom that he claimed was a freedom *for* rather than a freedom *from*. Biblical scholar Ernst Käsemann, in his aptly titled book *Jesus Means Freedom*, observes that "Jesus broke through the piety and theology of his contemporaries and brought God's promise and love in place of the Mosaic law, his own endowment with the Spirit in place of the Jewish tradition, clarity about God's will in place of casuistry, and grace in place of good works."[22] Jesus was able to embrace an order created out of freedom and for freedom. He was able to embrace an order without sacrificing the freedom to do so.

Play occurs in time and history but is not limited by time or history. "Play consists in part in processing memories. However, it can also mediate change, alter the present, and actualize the future because it does not depend on physical time or historical consciousness, even though it is not ahistorical in itself."[23] In Jesus' encounter with both devotees and detractors, he was able to bring change by playing through time and history. He was able to juxtapose playfully the past and the present and through them posit a hopeful future.

Perhaps the greatest example of a religious player in our time was Martin Luther King Jr. His ability to play within the overlapping spheres of American civil religion and African American spirituality allowed him to claim the freedom that presumably lay at the heart of each and to build a new order on the pillars of this freedom. It was this new order that constituted his powerful image of "the dream." King's model was Jesus, who was a player par excellence. Jesus showed the way to move nimbly through and around the religious authorities by being creative (liberating) within the spirit of the rules (law).

"So You Want to Play Rough, Eh?"

In the 1983 film *Scarface*, the main character, Tony Montana, utters this phrase. Scarface has become an important cultural icon for many rap artists and fans, inspiring posters, clothing, and many other references. For our purposes, however, it is this phrase that serves as a point of departure for our concluding observations on Jesus as a player. We have spoken of play as a form of evasion, delay, deception, and so on. There is a dimension of play that involves confrontation and even conflict. In this setting play becomes playfighting, rough play, or rough-and-tumble play.

A recent study examined the play practices of children and adolescents and found that "the case of rough-and-tumble play (R&T), or playfighting, seems particularly problematic."[24] The findings of this study suggest that rough play serves the purpose of establishing dominance, especially among males. Moreover, the difference between playfighting and real fighting substantially disappears. A line is crossed, and the quest for diversion becomes the intent to do harm to one's opponent.

Clifford Geertz developed the concept of deep play after observing gambling in cockfighting in Bali. The addition of violence (cockfighting) to play (gambling) creates a play of a different hue. Geertz observes that "Balinese go to cockfights to find out what a man, usually composed, aloof, almost obsessively self-absorbed, a kind of moral autocosm, feels like when attacked, tormented, challenged, insulted, and driven in result to the extremes of fury, he has totally triumphed or been brought fatally low."[25] This deep play has even more extreme manifestations, for example, in war. Warfare is sometimes referred to as *war games* and in some cultures is waged in a playful manner. When war, aggression, and violence are appended to the idea of play, as they are in certain video games, the playful manner in which this conflict is waged nearly obscures the fact that in war real people actually die.

> Play is training for the unexpected.
>
> *Marc Bekoff*
> *Contemporary American*
> *biologist*

The relationship between play and power is deeply rooted in Western ideology. Plato understood play as part of transcendental being, referring to an irreducible, immutable, abstract, and nonviolent interaction between the elements of reality. On the other hand, an alternative Hellenic notion of play linked it with competition, contest, and physical force. In the first, power is a transcendent principle, and in the second, power is a physical force. Mihai I. Spariosu notes that "from the very beginning the divided Hellenic notions of power, as well as their divided counterparts, the Hellenic notions of play, engage in a contest for cultural authority that has intermittently been carried on to the present day."[26] Brian Sutton-Smith argues that the relationship between play and power is rhetorical: "The rhetoric of play as power is about the use of play as the representation of conflict and as a way to fortify the status of those who control the play or are its heroes. This rhetoric is as ancient as warfare and patriarchy."[27] Deep play, power play, rough-and-tumble play, especially as exclusively male or patriarchal activities, are all dimensions of the serious side of play.

Jesus was engaged in cultural, political, and religious play in his day. But the significance of play in the activities of Jesus was not exhausted by these contexts. One would not ordinarily associate Jesus, play, and the cross. However, the cross is a symbol of what happens when play in any or all of the above contexts gets rough. That is, when one continually circumvents the cultural, political, and religious norms of the times, the stakes are increased. When the play gets rough, the "as if" dimension of play diminishes and play-fighting is indistinguishable from real violence. As noted above, the purpose of rough play is to establish dominance and to see what happens to a composed and collected individual when "attacked, tormented, challenged, and insulted"; to see whether the individual totally triumphs or is brought fatally low.

In the cross we see the ultimate example of rough play. Its brutality is combined with the macabre carnival that surrounded Roman crucifixions. It is both the occasion of the fatal disposition of Jesus and the occasion of his ultimate triumph. In the cross the play of Jesus amid the cultural, political, and religious powers of his time morphed into a cosmic encounter between good and

> When children pretend, they're using their imaginations to move beyond the bounds of reality. A stick can be a magic wand. A sock can be a puppet. A small child can be a superhero.
>
> *Fred Rogers*
> *American children's*
> *television host*
> *1928–2003*

evil. Yet Jesus is not defeated by the game but emerges victorious.

Play as a fundamentally human activity has a cultural, political, and religious meaning. Moreover, Jesus as "the Son of Man" or, more adequately translated, the "human one," can be seen as one who engages in this practice of play. Jesus was a player in that as a quintessential human one, he had the free will to freewheel in the world in which he found himself. Play is connected to free will because it means that the outcome is not predetermined. There is an element of joy in the exercise of free will. Free will is exercised within the boundaries of time and space established by God—in traditional theological language, with the providence of God.

4

the spirit at play: humanity, church, and the cosmos

As a young boy I had the pleasure of being the oldest of five children. I have two brothers and two sisters. We were the children of the pastor and first lady of the Second Gethsemane Missionary Baptist Church in Detroit, Michigan. Needless to say, we spent a great deal of our young lives in church. Sunday school began at 9:00 a.m. on Sunday mornings and was followed by morning worship at 11:00 a.m. Then there were frequent afternoon services, either at our church or at a neighboring congregation. And at least once a month we had an evening service. Added to these were the occasional "special teas," revivals, and anniversary celebrations.

Because we spent so much time in a worship context, one of our favorite pastimes was "playing church." This play involved taking on the roles and even the personae of adults in worship. I played the role of the preacher/pastor; the oldest of my brothers played the church musician; my sisters played the roles of ushers or choir members, reflecting the engendered division of labor in traditional churches; and my youngest brother played the role of the deacon. We spent hours refining our roles, perfecting intonations, gestures, gaits, and demeanors. While we never seemed to take our "playing church" as seriously as those adults whom we imitated, we were often, in a sense, transported into a spiritual realm in which what we were doing was real. This was playing church in a positive sense.

As we have noted, genuine play involves a sense of "as if." In the case described above, the "as if" is in search of the real. It is an "as if" without pretense.

This manner of playing church did two things. It rooted us deeply in a worship tradition to which we paid homage and respect through imitation. Our playing church was respectful. It also allowed us to imagine and even experience new and creative ways to be church. It freed us to build on that tradition. Playing church in a manner that respected the tradition yielded interesting, though not surprising, results. I eventually became a preacher and a pastor. My oldest brother became and still is an accomplished church musician. My youngest brother became and still is a lay leader in his church. Playing church in a manner that expanded and built upon the tradition also yielded new and surprising results. My youngest sister never became a choir member but is a leader and trustee in her congregation. My oldest sister became an ordained minister. Playing church did not confine us to the limits of our tradition but allowed us access to it. Playing church did not alienate us from the roots of our tradition but allowed us to draw creative sustenance from those roots.

> Play is our brain's favorite way of learning.
>
> *Diane Ackerman*
> *Contemporary American*
> *author*

The Spirit of Play

There is a kind of playing church that, while not universally condemned, is sometimes looked upon with suspicion. The root of this suspicion is that this kind of play does
not take church quite seriously enough. This is the kind of
playing church that we see caricatured in popular culture.
Indeed, one of the most ubiquitous targets for humor in
African American folklore is the preacher specifically and
the church in general. Maya Angelou, in her splendid auto-
biographical narrative *I Know Why the Caged Bird Sings*,
tells the story of playing church.[1] It is a story full of humor
and pathos. More recently, the popularity of playwright
and filmmaker Tyler Perry is built on his church-based
melodramas that were popular Sunday afternoon fare in
African American communities throughout the United
States. These stage plays often exploited popular stereo-
types of church folk to make their point. Consistently,
African American church life has been fertile ground for
humor and amusement in American entertainment.

Not all instances of playing church are positive. In
fact, in the African American community, a certain kind
of playing church is roundly condemned by the faithful.
This condemnation has nothing to do with lighthearted or
humorous portrayals of the church. Playing church in this
sense is a serious matter. It has to do with a certain kind
of *phoniness* in faith and witness. Playing church is what
Karl Barth condemned in his critique of the bourgeois
church in nineteenth-century Germany. Playing church
is what Frederick Douglass condemned in his critique of
the Christianity of the slaveholding class in nineteenth-
century America. Like all play, this sort of playing church
involved an "as if" factor. However, in this instance, the

"as if" holds at bay the real. In each of the above instances, playing church was the greatest of all apostasies.[2]

We began this journey by considering what it might mean to think of God as the origin, both temporally and spatially, of play. We then asked what it might mean to think of Jesus as a player in this special but also general sense. It remains to ask what it might mean to speak of the Holy Spirit as the spirit of play. I want to argue here that the Holy Spirit supports play at three different levels: humanity at play, the church at play, and the cosmos at play. At best, what follows will merely suggest what this kind of play will look like. But for the purposes of concluding our discussion on play as a religious practice, I want to assert that these three levels of play are important to our understanding of the theme.

The Christian at Play . . . Again

Play is a fundamental and existential practice of every individual in general and every Christian in particular. The fact that we were created with free will suggests that we were created to play. This is not to say that labor is not an integral part of life or that it cannot be a creative and fulfilling activity. But while in labor life's creative and redemptive dimensions are necessarily subordinate to its functional and productive dimensions, in play creativity, fulfillment, and even purposelessness are front and center. The spirit

> Culture arises and unfolds in and as play.
> *Johan Huizinga*
> *Dutch historian*
> *1872–1945*

that animates humanity is the spirit of play. This spirit is the source of our capacity to actualize our potential and to honor God fully. We are able to actualize our potential because we have freedom. As Sartre noted, "If man knows himself to be free and desires to use his freedom, then his activity is play."[3] Play also allows us to honor God properly because genuine praise is, characteristically, play.

> Play is the only way the highest intelligence of humankind can unfold.
>
> *Joseph Chilton Pearce*
> *Contemporary American*
> *scholar*

Here we should recall David's play before the Lord, discussed in the previous chapter.

Play as Religion

In essence, play is at the heart of our religious experience and practice. This is the argument of David L. Miller, among others. Miller acknowledges that for many people the idea of play and the idea of religion may appear unrelated at best or incompatible at worst. He observes that "to refer to play as the religion behind man's everyday existence is to imply a radical reformation in the history of religious consciousness."[4]

This radical reformation in the history of religious consciousness is required because religion is normally centered on explaining, justifying, or demonstrating "what is," whether through abstract reasoning or profound feeling. Play as religion, however, is not focused on "what is" but on "stepping out" from everyday reality into an alternate sphere of meaning. As one cultural anthropologist notes, "The capacity of play to transcend empirical understanding closely associates it with religion."[5] Hugo Rahner makes a similar claim in his seminal work *Man at Play*. There he suggests that what is needed is a *theologia ludens*, that is, a theological perspective that reexamines the nature of God, the human being, and the church in light of the idea of play.[6]

This relation between play and religion is profound and fundamental. Jürgen Moltmann argues that "religion does not at all and in every instance originate in human *need* but is actually more likely an outcome of *play, representation,* and *imagination.*"[7] That is, we do not practice religion because we must, but because we may. Moltmann goes on to relate the notion of play and liberation in religion. He argues that play provides "liberation from the bonds of the present system of living."[8] In Moltmann's theology sin takes the concrete historical form of oppression, and it is this sin that inhibits play. Therefore the believer is unable to play while under the power of sin, guilt, and hopelessness.

Redemption is the restoration of the freedom to play. This view reflects the affirmation that freedom is the foundation of play. It also suggests, however, that those who fear liberty are opposed to play. Play, in this sense, is not a practice that is possible only in an original innocence or only in a fully restored righteousness. Play happens in the interstices. As creations of God, we play precisely because we live in the space between a historical garden and a future paradise. In the historical garden play is unnecessary because the "as if" has not emerged, and in the future paradise play is meaningless because the "as if" now is.

The Church at Play

The spirit of play that animates us as human beings is also present in that collective body referred to as the church. The difficulty with this assertion is that the Holy Spirit is rarely associated with the notion of play and that the activity of the church is rarely referred to as play. Perhaps in response to the bacchanal frivolity of the surrounding cultures, the early church attempted to rid itself of any suggestion that it should not be taken seriously. Even in those moments when the playful nature of the church should be most evident, such as high praise, play is rarely the term that is used to describe these moments. The connection between the church, the Holy Spirit, and play is perhaps more clearly seen by cultural anthropologists than it is by theologians.

> It is in playing, and only in playing, that the individual child or adult is able to be creative and to use the whole personality, and it is only in being creative that the individual discovers the self.
>
> *D. W. Winnicott*
> *British pediatrician*
> *1896–1971*

Frank E. Manning in a fascinating study of a Bermudian church explores "pentecostalism as a form of play."[9] In his study of the symbolic presentation of this congregation, Manning makes several observations that can contribute to our understanding of the church at play. First, he notes that there is an acceptable, and even expected, playful dimension of worship in this setting. "The first hour of the service takes the form of a hootenanny. Led by the choir and the dozen musicians on stage, the congregation sing, clap, and occasionally dance as familiar hymns are repeated twenty times over."[10]

This festive and even carnival-like atmosphere supports the pastor in the role of jokester. Manning reports that "on one occasion, he joked about his recent conviction in court for a speeding violation by suggesting that 'a speeding demon' jumped on his foot and made him exceed the limit before he knew what he was doing."[11] On another occasion, when attempting to exorcise a young man who was more inebriated than possessed, the pastor, after watching the young man vomit, declared, "We really felt a gush of the Holy Spirit here tonight."[12] The playfulness of this situation allows the congregants to respond sympathetically to the young man's desire to give his life to God and to change his ways, and simultaneously to acknowledge the reality of the fact that, in the words of one parishioner, "he was really very drunk."[13]

> The true object of all human life is play.
>
> G. K. Chesterton
> British author
> 1874–1936

The second observation that Manning makes in this regard is that there is a connection between evangelism and entertainment. "The church service has two unambiguous aims: to evangelize the gospel of salvation and to serve as a form of entertainment. Ritual symbolism joins edification and enjoyment, hell-fire preaching and mundane joking, holiness and histrionics, solemn piety and profane humor. The duality of purpose is reflected in the standard answer that [respondents] gave for going to church: 'to have a good time in the Lord.'"[14] This connection between evangelism and entertainment alters the prevailing social order experienced by congregants in which churches are awash in their sobriety while the bars and clubs are confined by their frivolity. Here evangelism and entertainment are allowed to play with one another.

The third observation that Manning makes is that in Pentecostalism the Holy Spirit is powerfully associated with play. "Much of the symbolic dualism of Pentecostalism pivots on the Holy Ghost . . . the Holy Ghost is conceived in terms of both sanctity and buffoonery. He is both the most sacred and the most ludic personage of the Trinity."[15] The whole idea that the church should be at play flows counter to the ecclesial consciousness of most Christian traditions, especially those that have been influenced by puritanical strains.[16]

Playing the Notes

The framers of the Nicene Creed sought to answer the question, "What are the essential characteristics of the church?" Their response was that the church is "one, holy, catholic, and apostolic." These characteristics were referred to as *notae ecclesia*, or notes of the church. Where these notes or marks were present, there was the church. These notes or marks can be correlated to four equally important affirmations regarding the New Testament church—that the church is known by its *kerygma*, *koinonia*, *diakonia*, and *didache*, that is, its proclamation, fellowship, service, and teaching. The church's unity is in its proclamation of Jesus Christ; the church's sanctity is in its communal nature; the church's universality is in its service to others; and the church's apostolic mission is to teach the faith from generation to generation. I want to suggest that there is a ludic element not only to the symbolic expression of the life of the church but in its very essence.

It is possible, according to one theorist, that play has become the defining mythology of our time.[17] Whether this is a modern development is debatable, given the fundamental role of play in Western thought. However, if play is our mythology, then it should manifest itself in mythical categories. David L. Miller, drawing on the work of mythologist Joseph Campbell, argues that play has the fourfold function required of an effective mythology. Play has an aesthetic/spiritual function that creates a sense of awe and wonder. Play has a poetic/natural function that provides a better understanding of the world. Play has a metamorphic/social function that provides a creative framework for community. Play has a therapeutic/psychological function that provides an understanding of the human psyche.

These four marks of mythology provide a suggestive parallel to the notes or marks of the church described above. The proclamation of the church is aesthetic in that it creates a spiritual sense of awe and wonder that unites all who truly hear it. The service of the church is poetic in that it creates a better understanding of the natural world that we inhabit and makes that service universal. The fellowship of the church is metamorphic in that it creates a model for society as an organism and therefore embodies a kind of sanctity. The teaching of the church is therapeutic in that it provides an understanding of the human mind as a place where truth is received and passed on in a true apostolic succession.

If the notes of the church and the marks of an effective mythology of play can be correlated, is it then possible that play is at the heart of the essence of the church? I am arguing that such is the case. The *nota ecclesia* as traditionally understood is that the church is one, holy, catholic, and apostolic. However, these notes are not just what the church is but are the notes that the church plays. These notes are played in different combinations creating distinctive chords. These notes are played in different orders creating distinctive scales. This is essentially why authentic, genuine expressions of church can have different forms. The church's power is rooted in its ability to play its own notes.

Playing Church in Two Keys

What kind of play should the church be engaged in today? At the risk of oversimplification, I want to suggest that the church in the United States plays its notes in two dominant keys. In the Greco-Roman world games were defined in two distinct ways. The Greeks saw games as competition, and they were arranged for and focused on the competitors. They encouraged participation. This competition created a kind of empathy among the competitors. They understood the sacrifice involved in taking part in the games. They had mutual respect for one another. Paul used these games as an allegory for the Christian life.

> Now in myth and ritual the great instinctive forces of civilized life have their origin: law and order, commerce and profit, craft and art, poetry, wisdom and science. All are rooted in the primeval soil of play.
>
> *Johan Huizinga*
> *Dutch historian*
> *1872–1945*

The Romans saw games as spectacle and entertainment, and they were arranged and focused on the spectators. They encouraged detachment. This detachment made possible the brutality of the games. As the spectators were no longer able to feel the pain of the victims of the games, bloodlust reigned. The games also reinforced the social stratification present among the people. Paul saw these games as barbaric demonstrations of cruelty. Jürgen Moltmann observed that "modern dictators are fond of sponsoring sports events; they subsidize highly trained professionals with whom the people can identify and who can become an object of the people's pride."[18]

One of the ways to understand the differences between traditional churches and the so-called megachurches today can be cautiously drawn from this comparison. One could say that traditional churches have focused on participation in the life of the congregation, but that participation has gradually lost its ludic character, quickly becoming mere labor or tasks. It is easy for members of these churches to feel like alienated participants. One could say that megachurches have focused on the spectacle of worship, but that spectacle has lost its ludic character, quickly becoming merely a flat vista. It is easy for members of these churches to feel like detached spectators. In both of these cases, something essential can be restored by playing the church notes in a fuller harmony.

> Play has been man's most useful preoccupation.
>
> Frank Caplan
> Contemporary American author

The Cosmos at Play

Not only is the spirit of play present in the inner and public life of humanity and in the visible and invisible dimensions of the life of the church, but it is also present in the beginning and end of the cosmos. This notion that play is associated with the cosmos is behind the claim of Heraclitus in *Fragment 52* that "the course of the world is a child at play, moving figures on a board, back and forth; it is the kingdom of a child." The relationship between play and the cosmos is not just a Western idea. In Hinduism there is a term, *lila*, that describes everything that is, including the cosmos, as the outcome of creative play by the divine absolute.

> Children need the freedom and time to play. Play is not a luxury. Play is a necessity.
>
> *Kay Redfield Jamison*
> *Contemporary American*
> *professor of psychiatry*

In the reflections that follow, I want to explore the validity of some preliminary assumptions about the cosmos and play. The cosmos is characterized by randomness but not by chaos. It is defined by reason and not by caprice. Chaos is matter without form or rules. Caprice is action without intention or aim. Randomness continually creates and unveils new forms and new rules. Reason provides a morality to movement. Play is the primary principle of the cosmos. It is reason and randomness. Play balances form and freedom. The existence of God cannot be proven by appeal to "intelligent design" or reason, or disproven by appeal to "infinite variability" or randomness, but only celebrated in play. This balance of form and freedom in the cosmos is evident in the two ends of the cosmological spectrum: creation and consummation. The great cosmological questions are: "How did it all begin?" and "How will it all end?"

God, Creation, and Play

In the creation traditions of Christianity, the fact that at the heart of the cosmos is play has perhaps been obscured by the historical struggle between the affirmation that God is the creator of the material world and the affirmation that another divine creative principle was responsible for the creation of the cosmos. This alternate divine creative principle was known as the *demiurge*. While the full explication of the history of this principle would take us far beyond the scope of this analysis, it is important to note that the word "demiurge" actually means "public worker" or "skilled craftsman." This idea that creation involved work was picked up by Plato and others. Traditional Christianity sought to counter this emphasis on creation as a work that perhaps required some divine effort or some preexistent material on which to work by emphasizing the idea of *creation ex nihilo* or creation by fiat. God creates something out of nothing simply by saying, "Let it be." More recent Christian thinkers, myself among them, have argued that the recovery of the idea of God as worker or laborer can be helpful in understanding the acts of God.[19] However, even the notion of God as worker may not, by itself, paint the most complete picture of God's activity.

What sense does it make to think of the creative activity of God as play? James Weldon Johnson's poem "The Creation" depicts the creative activity of God in ludic terms. While a full exploration of the ludic dimensions of

> The creation of something new is not accomplished by the intellect but by the play instinct.
>
> *Carl Jung*
> *Swiss psychoanalyst*
> *1875–1961*

this poem must await another occasion, the images that the poet presents are of a smiling, whimsical God. While traditional readings of this poem often focus on the section that describes the creation of humanity, with its emphasis on worker imagery, the major portion of the poem describes a smiling and playful God. In the depiction of the creation of the cosmos, the ludic character of the poem comes through.[20] It may be more meaningful to speak of God's creative activity as play rather than work or abstract acting. Work implies necessity and constraint. Abstract action implies disconnection and caprice. Play, however, is desirable but not necessary. Play is connected but not capricious.

God, Consummation, and Play

In 1964 German theologian Jürgen Moltmann published his groundbreaking book *A Theology of Hope*. Here he argued that theology had traditionally adopted the notion of creation as its starting point for understanding the movement of God. In order to understand God in history, we must begin, he argues, with the end. Eschatology should be the point of departure for theology. In conversation with other German and European thinkers, he considered the meaning of hope in history. He concluded that God can be apprehended only in light of what can be rather than what already is. History correctly understood is full of possibility, potential, and novelty.

In 1972, in response to some of the criticism of *A Theology of Hope* and its stern demeanor, Moltmann explored the idea of play in *Theology of Play*. In this exploration Moltmann ends up approaching this same understanding of history but from a slightly different angle. He notes that

"Christian eschatology has never thought of the end of history as a kind of retirement or payday or accomplished purpose but has regarded it totally without purpose as a hymn of praise for unending joy. . . . In the Christian way of thinking the so-called final purpose of history is then no purpose at all."[21] The end of all things, then, is a state of being without purpose, freed from necessity, and free for wonder, awe, and adoration. The end of all things, then, is characterized by play.

There is a story, actually a plotline from the old *Twilight Zone* television series, that might help us put a period on this discussion of the spirit of play. In this story a gambler dies and upon opening his eyes finds himself in an environment in which everything is clean and white; he sees beautiful women who simply adorn the place, and he finally meets his host, who advises him that he may have whatever he wants simply for the asking. Thinking about his past life, he asks for a casino and one instantly appears. He enters the casino and sits down at a poker table. The dealer distributes the cards and the gambler finds that he has been dealt four aces and a joker, an unbeatable hand in poker. He is giddy with excitement. Collecting his winnings he moves to the roulette wheel and wins every round. He wins with the slot machines and at blackjack. No matter what game he plays, he wins. He grows despondent because there is no thrill in knowing that you are going to win all the time.

If you want to be creative, stay in part a child, with the creativity and invention that characterizes children before they are deformed by adult society.

Jean Piaget
Swiss philosopher
1896–1980

He summons his host and tells him that he appreciates his surroundings but does not know how or why, given his lifestyle, he got into heaven.

But winning all the time was no fun. He asks to leave heaven and go to "the other place." The host then reveals to the gambler that "this is the other place." The insight of this story is that our idea of heaven as a place where we always win the game may be wrong. Heaven is a place where the games have ended but the play never does.

postlude:
playing around the world

This brief study of play has pursued a modest goal: to understand play as a religious practice in a general American context and in, at critical points, a specific African American context. It is important to note, however, that play is not tied to the interests of the leisure class nor to the availability of leisure time. Play is a fundamental human practice that allows people to endure, manage, and even enjoy life. Play is free, creative, obedient, and loyal.

Play as a Global Practice

Play is a global practice. It is part of every human society. Like law, it is essential to any human community. What counts as play may vary widely from setting to setting, but every society must play. It is for this reason that we might pick up the discussion of the idea of play as a theological motif. During the 1970s considerable attention was given to idea of play in religion and theology. More recently, however, the conversation regarding play has gone on principally among anthropologists, sociologists, educators, philosophers, and others. Theologians should enter this conversation anew because play represents a universal, common, everyday practice. Thus, it can provide a footing for theology within the actual lives of actual people. It can provide a clear connection between the concerns of the theologian and those of her audience.

Since the publication of Hugo Rahner's *Man at Play*, the need for a theology of play has been acknowledged. However, the shape, tenor, and tone such a *theologia ludens* should take have yet to be defined fully in light of our postmodern, late-imperial dissatisfaction with a life centered only around leisure. As baby boomers in the United States reach retirement age, there is no universal desire to center one's life around unending leisure (no matter how attractive this sounds during a stressful workday). The distinction between leisure as the absence of creative activity and play as supremely creative must be more clearly drawn. Many baby boomers want to stay in the game longer than their parents. They want to continue to play. In poorer nations and cultures, contact with affluent cultures increases curiosity about and desire to play. Play in its various cultural, political, and even religious settings will compel a new theology of play to be more global.

A New Theology of Play

We can make two concluding observations about the prospect of a new theology of play. First, play has to be taken seriously as a theological subject matter. David L. Miller offers this observation about a theology of play: "It is not therefore enough for a *theologia ludens* to be a theology about play, interpreting traditional doctrines of the faith *sub specie ludi*. At least this is not enough if a *theologia ludens* is to avoid being inadvertently a ludicrous theology.

Something more is needed. It must not only be *about* play; it must also be a theology *of* play, *by* play, and *for* play."[1] Although written decades ago, this fundamental observation about a theology of play must be part of any new manifestation thereof.

Second, play is not a foreign subject matter for theology. In fact, an authentic understanding of theology must acknowledge its playful essence. Jürgen Moltmann offers this observation: "On first glance, *Christian theology* is indeed the *theory of a practice* that alleviates human need: the theory of preaching, of ministries and services. But on second glance Christian theology is also an abundant rejoicing in God and the *free play* of thoughts, words, images, and songs with the grace of God."[2]

We live in a world marked by fabulous wealth and crushing poverty; magnificent medical advances and death by ancient plagues; remarkable greed and even more remarkable sacrifice. However, if we have been correct in our assertions in this book, then the recovery of play is a first step in reclaiming our freedom and recognizing our humanity. I see what it means to live in this primal freedom and humanity as I watch our fourteen-month-old grandson, Christian James, sprint with no particular destination with his arms out, his head thrown back, and irresistible laughter signifying his joy. As a theologian, I can respond only with an invitation. "Let's play!"

notes

Chapter 1. The Play's the Thing

1. The scholarly literature on the idea of play is voluminous, so this overview in no way pretends to be comprehensive. The thinkers here are presented because their work is foundational to the field and because there are elements within their work that contribute to answering the three major questions this project attempts to answer. One further caveat is in order. A great deal of the research on play takes animals and children as major subjects. For a good example of research on play and development in children, see Catherine Garvey, *Play* (Cambridge: Harvard University Press, 1977), and Jerome S. Bruner et al., eds., *Play: Its Role in Development and Evolution* (New York: Basic, 1976). Chapter 3 of Garvey's text presents an example of research on play in animals. For our purposes, however, the operative notion of play is one that is primarily related to the mature and generally human task of navigating one's way through the world as we know it.

2. Karl Groos, *The Play of Man* (New York: D. Appleton, 1916), 2.

3. Johan Huizinga, *Homo Ludens: A Study of the Play Element in Culture* (Boston: Beacon, 1955), 3.

4. Ibid., 4.

5. Ibid., 173.

6. Roger Callois, *Man, Play, and Games* (New York: Free Press of Glencoe, 1961), 9.

7. Brian Sutton-Smith, *The Ambiguity of Play* (Cambridge: Harvard University Press, 1977), vii.

8. Brian Sutton-Smith, "Recapitulation Redressed," in Jaipaul L. Roopnarine, ed., *Conceptual, Social-Cognitive, and Contextual Issues in the Fields of Play* (Westport, Conn.: Ablex, 2002), 7.

9. Ibid., 17.

10. Brian Sutton-Smith, ed., *Play and Learning* (New York: Gardner, 1979), 308.

11. See M. J. Ellis, *Why People Play* (Englewood Cliffs, N.J.: Prentice-Hall, 1973); Susanna Millar, *The Psychology of Play* (Baltimore: Penguin, 1968); Mihai I. Spariosu, *Dionysus Reborn: Play and the Aesthetic Dimension in Modern Philosophical and Scientific Discourse* (Ithaca, N.Y.: Cornell University Press, 1989); David Cohen, *The Development of Play* (Washington Square: New York University Press, 1987).

12. The most influential and fascinating treatment of the idea of mimesis is developed by Erich Auerbach in *Mimesis: The Representation of Reality in Western Literature* (Princeton: Princeton University Press, 1953). This work is based largely on a comparison of the ways that the world is represented in two classic texts; Homer's *Odyssey* and the Bible. In short, the former represents the world in "fully externalized description, uniform illustration, uninterrupted connection, free expression, all events in the foreground, displaying unmistakable meanings, few elements of historical development and of psychological perspective." The latter represents the world through description in which "certain parts brought into high relief, others left obscure, abruptness, suggestive influence of the unexpressed, 'background' quality, multiplicity of meanings and the need for interpretation, universal-historical claims, development of the concept of the historically becoming, and preoccupation with the problematic." In essence, the Bible rather than ancient Greek tragedy allows room for play. This element of mimesis is clearly evident in its connection to ludology, the study of games and especially video games, where the level of complexity is what makes the game "lifelike."

Chapter 2. Playing in the Dark

1. Mihai I. Spariosu, *The Wreath of Wild Olive: Play, Liminality, and the Study of Literature* (Albany, N.Y.: SUNY Press, 1977).

2. Ibid., 33.

3. Ibid., 34–35.

4. Toni Morrison, *Playing in the Dark: Whiteness and the Literary Imagination* (New York: Random, 1992), viii.

5. Ibid., 5.

6. Ibid., 7.

7. Ibid., 9.

8. Ibid., 17.

9. Ibid., 90.

10. Ibid., 4.

11. Joseph Conrad, *Heart of Darkness* (New York: Penguin, 1981), 9.

12. Ibid., 10.

13. Ibid., 31.

14. Ibid., 95.

15. Ibid., 24.

16. Ibid., 51.

17. Ibid., 87.

18. Ibid., 52–53.

19. Ibid., 65.

20. Riggins R. Earl Jr., *Dark Symbols, Obscure Signs: God, Self, and Community in the Slave Mind* (Maryknoll, N.Y.: Orbis, 1993).

21. Ibid., 149.

22. Ibid., 150.

23. Ibid., 154.

24. Dwight N. Hopkins, *Down, Up, and Over: Slave Religion and Black Theology* (Minneapolis: Fortress Press, 2000), 51.

25. While it can be argued that the Puritans did engage in their own kind of play, it remains my conviction that the puritanical principle was one of work as a primary creative and redemptive activity.

26. Hopkins, *Down, Up, and Over,* 114.

27. Ibid., 116.

28. Ibid., 117.

29. Ibid., 119.

30. George Herbert Mead, *Play, School, and Society*, ed. Mary Jo Deegan (New York: Peter Lang, 1999), liii. Mead is perhaps best known for his classic work, *Mind, Self and Society*, ed. Charles Morris (Chicago: University of Chicago Press, 1934). For the purposes of this chapter, see also his "The Relation of Play to Education," *University Record*, Chicago 1 (May 22, 1896): 141–45.

31. Quoted in Mead, *Play, School, and Society*, lxxvi. Dewey was a prolific writer and is perhaps best known for his work *School and Society* (Chicago: University of Chicago Press, 1900). For the purposes of this chapter, see also his "Play" in *A Cyclopedia of Education*, vol. 4, ed. Paul Monroe (New York: Macmillan, 1913), 725–27.

32. Quoted in Mead, *Play, School, and Society*, xc. Addams is perhaps best known for *Twenty Years at Hull House* (New York: Macmillan, 1910). For the purposes of this chapter, see also her "Work and Play as Factors in Education," *Chautauquan* 42 (November 1905): 251–55.

33. Bernard Mergen, *Play and Playthings: A Reference Guide* (Westport, Conn.: Greenwood, 1982).

34. Ibid., 39.

35. Ibid., 51.

36. Brian Sutton-Smith, *The Ambiguity of Play* (Cambridge: Harvard University Press, 1977), 9.

37. Zora Neale Hurston, *Their Eyes Were Watching God* (Urbana: University of Illinois Press, 1978), 30.

38. Ibid., 44.

39. Ibid., 46.

40. Ibid., 124.

41. Ibid., 146.

42. Ibid., 155.

43. Ibid., 161.

44. Ibid., 167.

45. Ibid., 169.

46. Ibid., 210.

47. Ibid., 171.

48. Ibid., 187.

49. Ibid., 192.

50. Ibid., 194.

51. Ibid., 199.

52. Ibid., 200.

53. Ibid., xv.

54. Ibid., 236.

55. Baseball fields are an interesting combination of both uniformity and variety. Individual ballparks may differ as in the cases of Fenway Park in Boston and Wrigley Field in Chicago, among many others. However, within each ballpark the height of the pitcher's mound and the distance between the bases are the same.

56. In fact, there is actually no playtime that is unlimited. However, the notion of an endless playtime has been associated with the emergence of a leisure class. The fantasy of endless leisure is, however, only available for an elite few. Perhaps this is a factor in the popularity of cricket (which can go on for days) and tennis among the elite.

Chapter 3. Don't Hate the Player, Hate the Game

1. Roger Callois, *Man, Play, and Games* (New York: Free Press of Glencoe, 1961), viii.

2. Mihai I. Spariosu, *Dionysus Reborn: Play and the Aesthetic Dimension in Modern Philosophical and Scientific Discourse* (Ithaca, N.Y.: Cornell University Press, 1989), 20.

3. For an excellent summary of the major issues in Christology, see Alister E. McGrath, *The Christian Theology Reader* (Oxford: Blackwell, 2001).

4. See G. E. Lessing's "On the Proof of Spirit and Power" for the full discussion.

5. Peter L. Berger, *The Heretical Imperative* (New York: Doubleday, 1980).

6. Jaroslav Pelikan, *Jesus through the Centuries: His Place in the History of Culture* (New York: Harper, 1987).

7. Jaipaul L. Roopnarine, ed., *Conceptual, Social-Cognitive, and Contextual Issues in the Fields of Play* (Westport, Conn.: Ablex, 2002), 4.

8. Ibid.

9. See my *We Shall All Be Changed: Social Transformation and Theological Renewal* (Minneapolis: Fortress Press, 1997), where I argue that Jesus in his own way resisted and overcame the honor/shame complex.

10. deSilva, David A. Honor, *Patronage, Kinship, and Purity: Unlocking New Testament Culture* (Downers Grove, Ill.: InterVarsity, 2000), 25.

11. Roopnarine, *Conceptual . . . Issues* 5.

12. Ralph Abernathy, "Leisure Time for the Poor," *Spectrum* 48 (January–February 1972): 11–12, 14.

13. Evans, *We Shall All Be Changed.* See the section on honor and shame for a description of the role of grace in mitigating the deleterious effects of this cultural system.

14. Jerome S. Bruner et al., eds., *Play* (New York: Basic, 1976), 166.

15. Brian Sutton-Smith, ed., *Play and Learning* (New York: Gardner, 1979).

16. Cited in Robert K. Johnston, *The Christian at Play* (Grand Rapids: Eerdmans, 1983), 38.

17. Ibid., 36.

18. See John Dominic Crossan, *God and Empire: Jesus against Rome, Then and Now* (New York: HarperCollins, 2007). See also Richard A. Horsley, *Jesus and Empire: The Kingdom of God and the New World Disorder* (Minneapolis: Fortress Press, 2003).

19. Matthew 12:1-12; Mark 2:23–3:4; Luke 6:1-9; and John 5:9-18.

20. Johnston, *Christian at Play*, 41.

21. Rubem A. Alves, *Tomorrow's Child: Imagination, Creativity, and the Rebirth of Culture* (New York: Harper, 1972), 93.

22. Ernst Käsemann, *Jesus Means Freedom* (Philadelphia: Fortress Press, 1969), 10.

23. Ruth E. Burke, *The Games of Poetics: Ludic Criticism and Postmodern Fiction* (New York: Peter Lang, 1994), 26.

24. Anthony D. Pellegrini, "Perceptions of Playfighting and Real Fighting: Effects of Sex and Participant Status," in Roopnarine, *Conceptual . . . Issues*, 223–34.

25. Clifford Geertz, *The Interpretation of Culture* (New York: Basic, 1973), 27.

26. Mihai I. Spariosu, *Dionysus Reborn: Play and the Aesthetic Dimension in Modern Philosophical and Scientific Discourse* (Ithaca, N.Y.: Cornell University Press, 1989), 6.

27. Brian Sutton-Smith, *The Ambiguity of Play* (Cambridge: Harvard University Press, 1997), 10.

Chapter 4: The Spirit at Play

1. Maya Angelou, *I Know Why the Caged Bird Sings* (New York: Random, 1969).

2. *Apostasy* (Greek *apostasia*, "insurrection"), the total abandonment of Christianity by a baptized person. In the early church it was considered one of the three unpardonable sins, with the other two being murder and fornication. Apostasy is to be distinguished from laxity in the practice of religion and from heresy, the formal denial of one or more doctrines of the Christian faith. In Roman Catholic canon law, the term also refers to the abandonment of the religious state by a monk or nun who has taken perpetual vows and leaves the religious life without the appropriate dispensation. The word *apostasy* also can be used to describe the rejection of any religious faith.

3. Cited in Jürgen Moltmann, *Theology of Play* (New York: Harper, 1972), 21.

4. David L. Miller, *God and Games: Toward a Theology of Play* (New York: Harper, 1970), 154.

5. Frank E. Manning, "The Rediscovery of Religious Play: A Pentecostal Case," in David F. Lancy and B. Allan Tindall, eds., *The Anthropological Study of Play: Problems and Prospects* (Cornwall: Leisure, n.d.), 145.

6. Hugo Rahner, *Man at Play* (New York: Herder, 1967).

7. Moltmann, *Theology of Play*, 57.

8. Ibid., 13.

9. Manning, "Rediscovery of Religious Play," 140.

10. Ibid.

11. Ibid., 141.

12. Ibid., 143.

13. Ibid., 144.

14. Ibid.

15. Ibid.

16. "It was the Protestant Reformation that severed the two, stigmatizing play as a sinful waste of time and idealizing ascetic rationality as the model of ethical behavior." Ibid., 145.

17. Miller, *God and Games.*

18. Moltmann, *Theology of Play,* 7.

19. See my *We Have Been Believers: An African American Systematic Theology* (Minneapolis: Fortress Press, 1992).

20. James Weldon Johnson, *God's Trombones* (New York: Viking, 1927).

21. Moltmann, *Theology of Play,* 34, 36.

Postlude: Playing around the World

1. David L. Miller, *God and Games: Toward a Theology of Play* (New York: Harper, 1970), 159.

2. Jürgen Moltmann, *Theology of Play* (New York: Harper, 1972), 27.

suggestions for further reading

The titles listed here serve as suggestions for further reading and also as a background to the ideas the author worked with in writing this book.

Roger Callois. *Man, Play and Games* Urbana and Chicago: University of Illinois Press, 1961. Translated by Meyer Barash. Callois draws upon the work of Huizinga, providing a systematic approach to the concept of play. Callois was a French intellectual whose idiosyncratic scholarship draws upon philosophy, literary criticism, and sociology, among other disciplines.

Joseph Conrad. *Heart of Darkness.* J.M. Dent, London: Orion Publishing Group, 1899. Conrad was a Polish-born British novelist noted as a precursor of the modernist movement in literature. His novels explore the depths and complexities of the human soul.

Riggins R. Earl, Jr. *Dark Symbols, Obscure Signs: God, Self and Community in the Slave Mind.* Maryknoll, New York: Orbis Books, 1993. Earl is a theologian whose work focuses on the ethical dimensions of the experience of enslaved Africans in the New World. This text explores the place of multivalent signs and symbols in the construction of the ethos of black life.

Dwight Hopkins. *Down, Up, and Over: Slave Religion and Black Theology*. Minneapolis: Fortress Press, 2000. Hopkins is a theologian whose constructive work has focused on mining the depths of the experience of enslaved Africans as expressed in that collection of materials referred to as slave narratives. In this work he explores the notion of "sunup to sundown" as that period of time the lives of enslaved Africans belonged to their owners, and "sundown to sunup" as that period of time they could call their own.

Johan Huizinga. *Homo Ludens: A Study of the Play-Element in Culture*. Boston: Beacon Press, 1950. Huizinga was a Dutch historian whose training was in medieval and renaissance studies. In this classic text he explores the fertile possibility that play is the primary formative element in human culture.

Jürgen Moltman. *Theology of Play*. New York: Harper and Row, 1972. Moltmann is a German Protestant theologian whose most well-known work is *Theology of Hope* (1967). In this text he responds to criticism that he view of theology is devoid of a sense of joy by exploring the more playful aspects of theology.

reader's guide

Following are some questions for consideration in individual or group discussion:

What is the relationship between play and games? Do you notice places in our culture where the element of actual play is lost because the games mimic real life so closely?

What are the major differences between play as seen in wealthier societies and play in poorer societies? One of the major obstacles to the continuing importance of play in our time is its association with "mere leisure." How is play related, if at all, to leisure?

What have been the distinctive characteristics of play in African American culture? Among marginalized and oppressed populations, play has often been the most misunderstood cultural practice.

Why is the element of play absent from so much of our religious practice and theological reflection? How can a broadened and deepened understanding of play help us to recover hidden theological insights and enrich impoverished religious practices?